WHEN SUCCESS IS A CRIME

WHEN SUCCESS IS A CRIME

VIOLATION OF HUMAN RIGHTS TO ISAIAS FAMILY IN ECUADOR

Second Edition

ALBERTO VALENCIA GRANADA

Alexandria Library
MIAMI

ISBN: 978-1514220740

Library of Congress Control Number: 2011910169

www.alexlib.com

The ultimate tragedy is not the oppression and cruelty by the bad people but the silence over that by the good people.

Martin Luther King Jr.

He who allows an injustice to occur opens the way for other injustices.

Willy Brandt

CONTENTS

INTRODUCTION

From the Ecuadorian financial crisis of 1998-1999 through the past decade, the "Filanbanco Case," or the story of the Isaias Group, has been filled with political persecution, pettiness and envy on the part of politicians, Presidents of the Republic, entrepreneurs, media owners, public officials and the offices of the Judicial Branch entrusted with imparting justice.

The politicization of justice and the violation of due process are evident in the case of the entrepreneurs of the Isaias family and speak of a State in which the division of powers or the checks and balances, such as those in the U.S., do not work, and where there is no respect for the human rights enshrined in fundamental principles, such as the tenet that everyone has the right to a fair trial. These legal aspects that have formed part of the actions against the Isaias' are amply addressed in this work.

The author also analyzes the climate of the economic crisis experienced in Ecuador between 1998 and 1999, which drove more than 20 banks to insolvency and led the Isaias Group to make the decision to turn Filanbanco over to the Ecuadorian government on December 2nd of 1998. He also highlights the success story of a financial empire founded in 1915 with the opening of a grocery store in the small village of Catarama by Mr. Emi-

11

lio Isaias, a Lebanese immigrant. Thanks to the entrepreneurial vision, the dedication, the sacrifice and loyalty passed down from generation to generation, the Isaias family was able to build one of the strongest and most diversified financial groups in Ecuador.

Through the Nahim Isaias Foundation, which provides numerous health, education and cultural programs for thousands of Ecuadorians of limited financial means, the Isaias Group brought social responsibility and commitment to its business successes, qualities that, unfortunately, are not a constant in our companies.

However, the generosity of the Group, its investments in Ecuador, its contributions to economic development in various sectors and the cutting-edge technology it applied in its companies were overshadowed by the characteristic Latino envy of success on the part of politicians and commercial competitors. This is pointed out by Miguel Davila, the Superintendent of Banks, who was responsible for the decision to close Filanbanco in July of 2001, after it was already under government control, when the poor management and corruption of the Deposit Guarantee Agency (AGD) administrators led to its ruin. In an interview granted to Ramon Jimeno in 2006, Davila responded to the following question:

R.J: *"In the case of Ecuador and the country's economy, how do you rate the impact on the courts of the political instability and constant changes in the government?"*

M.D. *"Let's see, perhaps it would be better to back up a bit. I would like to begin by stating my opinion that this expatriation of investors and Ecuadorian business owners came about for legal reasons, legal uncertainty, but it also came about, perhaps primarily, due to a poor business environment that has almost become a part of our Ecuadorian culture. That is, here in this country, if someone is successful in business, this doesn't motivate others to go into business looking for success, as well, but rather elicits envy and a desire to ruin that person..."* Really, outside of envy and the desire to do moral and financial harm to the Isaias Group, there is no other explanation as to why, after 10 years, this clear case of a false accusation has not yet been resolved by the Ecuadorian justice system.

PROLOGUE

I feel honored to have been invited to write a few lines to introduce this new work of Alberto Valencia, the distinguished Colombian academic, sociologist, political scientist and researcher. In it, the author deals with an underlying theme that is of great importance and relevance in our region: the respect for human rights and the administration of justice.

In effect, relating the case and the hardships that affected a prominent family of Ecuadorian bankers and businessmen of Lebanese descent, who created a powerful financial group from scratch, he exposes the shortcomings of the justice system and the unacceptable interference of politics in its decisions.

Beyond the story of the Isaias family's tribulations, achievements and financial prowess, which were the fruit of the efforts and entrepreneurial spirit of three generations, he demonstrates, without sugar-coating, how the democratic and judicial institutions function in some of our countries. In many cases, they are a burden to development, as they do not create an environment that favors investment and the type of entrepreneurship displayed by the Isaias'.

In spite of the ill-fated experiments of the past, which only produced economic recession and depression, there are still countries in the Americas that insist on rehashing schemes and policies that were, are and always will be a failure wherever they are attempted. Likewise, the respect for human rights, the rule of the law over arbitrariness and abuse of power, the independence of the Judicial Branch, the observance of due process, the presumption of innocence and the statute of limitations are all pillars of the State, of the law and of democracy.

For all of the above reasons, works like this one by Alberto Valencia merit special attention, as they perform the valuable service of reporting the violations and irregularities that corrupt our national institutions.

Juan Larrain
Miami, November of 2010.

Ambassador Larrain served as the Permanent Representative of Chile in the United Nations from 1994 to 2000. He also represented his country in the Council on Security (1996-1997). Prior to his service in the United Nations, Mr. Larrain was the General Chilean Consul in New York and the Secretary of the Chilean Embassy in London, Washington and the OAS.

1

FILANBANCO: POLITICAL PERSECUTION AND PETTINESS IN THE ACTION AGAINST THE ISAIAS BUSINESS GROUP

By way of introduction

After ten years of residence in Miami, joined by hundreds of Latin American citizens from various countries for whom political persecution and the violation of human rights left no other option but exile, leaving their land, their property and their most cherished possessions behind, the brothers Roberto and William Isaias Dassum wait for the conclusion of a penal process known as the "Filanbanco Case," marked by political persecution on the part of directors, judges and magistrates and pettiness on the part of the majority of the media, which is responsible for influencing public opinion by propagating a perception of guilt and condemnation for an alleged crime of "bank embezzlement."

In order for Roberto and William Isaias to have committed this supposed "bank embezzlement," they would have had to misuse the funds loaned to Filanbanco by the Central Bank of Ecuador or misuse public funds in some other way. Since December 2nd of 1998, the day on which Filanbanco was turned over to the Ecuadorian

State, the most incredible examples of politicization of justice have been demonstrated on the part of officials of the Judicial Branch and the Executive Branch, in order to take actions against a solid Ecuadorian financial group that was an exemplary model of strength and trustworthiness in the country. This story, which has yet to end, demonstrated the highest degree of hatred and vengefulness against the Group in 2008, when more than 150 companies were seized by the State under the false pretenses of compensating accountholders for damages arising from the closure of Filanbanco under government control.

In 1960, the Isaias family acquired La Filantropica Savings and Credit, which later became Filanbanco, and within three decades, it was transformed into the largest and most modern bank in Ecuador. In the late 90's, as Latin America was facing capital flight from the Region following the East Asian and Russian Crises, Ecuador experienced a political-economic crisis, caused initially by its military confrontation with Peru and aggravated by the lack of sufficient hydroelectric energy production due to low water levels, followed by the agricultural difficulties caused by the severe El Niño phenomenon. These factors deepened the internal political crisis that destabilized the country, which had four Presidents of the Republic within a period of eight years. The economic crisis primarily affected the sectors of agricultural and aquaculture exports located in coastal areas, which were the bank's principle credit recipients. The cessation of payments from these sectors and the restrictions placed on Ecuador's international lines of credit for financing new and existing operations gave rise to an insolvency problem in Filanbanco, which was managed by tapping into the resources of other companies within the Group and through liquidity loans from the Central Bank of Ecuador, in accordance with existing regulations at that time.

As Ecuador's financial crisis deepened, and the bank maintained it operations keeping open all of its branches, the liquidity problem persisted, and Filanbanco had reached its liquidity advance loan limit with the Central Bank that rose to 425 million dollars, which were used basically to fund domestic withdrawals and payments to international bank's credit operations., the shareholders decided to turn the bank over to the Ecuadorian Government on December 2nd of 1998, through a new Deposit Guarantee Agency (AGD),

The Agency froze access to all deposits in March 1999 thereafter intervened several banks and gradually restored the functioning of the financial system. External audits of all banks where commissioned by AGD, and after receiving the audit results, only 21 banks reopened from the 38 then existing banks.

Filanbanco, having paid to all his clients during the private administration crisis, and due to the restored financial stability , saw most of its clientele returning to the bank. Only six months later, in May of 1999, according to the report submitted by ING Barings, the investment bank contracted to restructure and then sell the bank, Filanbanco had generated a hundred million dollars in profits and was ready to be reprivatized. Going against the advice of ING Barings, financial experts and financiers, who all recommended selling Filanbanco at that time, and due that the Central bank could no longer act as lender of last resort, the Government converted Filanbanco in a "bank of banks" with the mission of saving certain financial institutions of interest to the government; the AGD turned Filanbanco over to the Ministry of Finances and the bank was obligated to authorize huge loans to other banks, to redeem Certificates of Restructuring (CDR's) issued by other financial institutions for amounts far beyond its means, and to merge with La Previsora Bank to prevent the latter's insolvency. In April of 2001, crippled by the poor administrative decisions of the authorities, which closed it in July of that same year.

Up to this point, there is nothing unusual about this story. The closure of a bank, whether privately owned or State owned, is not an extraordinary occurrence in countries where the Banking Superintendence or other similar institution acts in accordance with the law. Even in Ecuador in 1999, when the crisis obligated the closure of many other banks, only the owner of Progreso Bank had legal problems when it was proven that the bank had made loans to affiliates in an amount above that which was permitted by law. The absurd part is that, two years later, the head of the Superintendence of Banks at that time requested that the Attorney General carry out an investigation and subsequently file charges of "bank embezzlement" for the alleged misuse of funds advanced by the Central Bank of Ecuador to Filanbanco between September 24th and December 2nd of 1998, even though reports, both from that time and subsequently, stated the contrary.

The Filanbanco Case is especially moving and significant because of the political persecution, personal intrigue and intentional mismanagement, on the part of the Attorney General, the Supreme Court of Justice and the Presidency of the Republic, in what has become for Ecuadorians the most emblematic criminal trial in the country's history, which, after ten years, has yet to be resolved in accordance with due process.

First, we should point out the unusual legal treatment of the case from the very beginning. The businessmen, Roberto and William Isaias, were charged by the Attorney General in June of 2000 for the alleged crime of "bank embezzlement," which did not even exist in the Ecuadorian Penal Code until May of 1999.

Within this framework of persecution, which has no legal precedent in any country where there is a division of powers, certain laws were enacted and others reformed for the sole purpose of applying them against Roberto and William Isaias. Law No. 99-26, which amends the General Law of Institutions in the Financial System, added a third paragraph to Article 257 of the Penal Code, introducing the new crime of "bank embezzlement."

Extradition Law No. 2000-24 was amended in detriment to the Isaias brothers, establishing that, in order to initiate an Active Extradition process, an order for preventative custody or an executable sentence was required. The previous law did not include this order for preventative custody, which was subsequently issued against the Isaias'.

However, the most evident violation of the Universal Declaration of Human Rights with regard to the rules of due process and the presumption of innocence is found in Constituent Mandate

No. 13, enacted on July 9th of 2008 in a plenary session of the Constituent Assembly. This mandate ratified the validity of Decision AGD-UIO-2008-12, which initiated the seizure of the Isaias Group's companies. Mandate No. 13 stated that this Decision was not subject to protection under the Constitution or of any other special nature, and that any motion for such protection would be filed without prejudice to the fulfillment of the Decision. Any judge or magistrate petitioned to hear and rule on these motions would have to make them inadmissible under penalty of removal from office, without prejudice to any related criminal liability.

As if that were not enough, Executive Decree No. 914 amended the regulations of the Law on Travel Documents. It was enacted on February 18th of 2008 after William Isaias had presented his passport in the Ecuadorian Consulate in Miami on January 29th of 2008. William Isaias' old and new passports were both illegally retained. This Decree ordered that the Ministry of Foreign Relations, its departments and consulate offices abstain from authorizing passports to Ecuadorians that were fugitives from justice, and in order to facilitate the identification of those citizens, the Ministry of Governance and Policies would provide a list with their names, copies of the court orders and other relevant information.

Secondly, the politicization of justice in the case of the Isaias brothers has hindered the application of due process. Twenty-four Supreme Court Justices, eight Chief Justices of the Supreme Court and six constitutionally elected Presidents have been involved in the case. The Attorney General, more than two-and-a-half years after filing charges of "bank embezzlement," after new investigations, comparison of documents and receipt of new statements, dismissed the embezzlement charges in November of 2002, but sustained other minor infractions that, according to the law, were subject to bail. The Chief Justice of the Supreme Court illegally disregarded the Attorney General's decision, and four months later – in March of 2003 – called for a full trial of the Isaias Dassum brothers.

The most irrefutable example of manipulation of justice in order to prevent the Isaias' from being declared innocent, in spite of all the evidence in their favor, was the dismissal of the Supreme Court of Justice on December 9th of 2004 by President Lucio Gutierrez. The President, who at that time was politically crippled and on the brink of removal from office, decided that rumors that the Criminal Chambers of the Court would absolve the Isaias' provided a good excuse for dismissing the entire Supreme Court and increasing his popularity at the expense of the much talked about

Filanbanco Case. In this way, any possibility for a fair trial was eliminated.

Thirdly, many entrepreneurs in the financial, commercial and industrial sectors, as well as in the media, had acted in an opportunistic fashion and in poor faith during the ensuing 10 years. All of these have been more determined to eliminate a strong business competitor with the government's help than to demonstrate their solidarity. They have all helped to propagate the false notion among the Ecuadorian people that the Isaias Group was responsible for the economic crisis experienced by the country between 1998 and 1999, ignoring the global nature of the crisis that was much more marked in certain Asian and Latin American countries. The information has been manipulated to such an extent that the fact has been repeatedly obscured that the closure of Filanbanco happened while it was under government control, as a result of administrative errors and poor management that touch more upon the Penal Code than the Financial Code.

Lastly, the "Filanbanco Case," or the political persecution against the Isaias Business Group, is significant because it deals with one of the most important financial groups in Ecuador, a financial empire that was forged through decades of laborious effort on the part of three generations with faith in Ecuador's progress, initiated in 1912 when

Mr. Emilio Isaias, as he was registered in Spanish, reached port after a three-month voyage on a boat originating from the Lebanese town of Sequiet Eljait. When he settled in the town of Catarama, in his pockets, Mr. Isaias had what would be the equivalent of 1,000 dollars today.

As the Isaias Group grew financially, it did not forget its social and cultural commitment to the Ecuadorian people. Through the Nahim Isaias Foundation, it has performed true humanitarian work for more than four decades, through medical centers and educational and cultural programs for the lowest-income population, programs that were generally not covered by the State.

When governments do not send a clear message of economic and commercial security and when populism comes at the expense of entrepreneurs, this not only frightens off investors, but also motivates many businessmen to invest their capital abroad. For now, Miami is one of the main destinations for Latin American business owners that do not have these guarantees in their country and that have emigrated, along with their capital.

2
THE ECONOMIC CRISIS IN ECUADOR 1998-1999

Blaming Filanbanco for the crisis is simply an attempt to cover up the government's responsibility

Since Filanbanco was turned over to the Ecuadorian government in December of 1998 and was closed under its control in July of 2001, the government and most of the media, which was aware that the Isaias Group controlled the competition, have made great efforts for over a decade to propagate the notion among the Ecuadorian people that the Isaias Group was responsible for the economic crisis experienced by the country between 1998 and 1999, ignoring the global nature of the crisis that was much more marked in certain Asian and Latin American countries. The information has been manipulated to such an extent that the fact has been repeatedly obscured that the closure of Filanbanco happened while it was under government control, as a result of administrative errors and poor management that touch upon the Penal Code.

Historically, Ecuador, like the majority of Latin American countries, has demonstrated high rates of social inequality, urban unemployment and illiteracy, scant institutional development and severe political instability. Given these characteristics, it was much more difficult to face the economic crisis of 1998-1999, which was the result of a series of events that had been set in motion years earlier.

Ecuador took advantage of its oil resources in order to support the known model of economic development, Import-Substituting Industrialization (ISI), but by the 80's, just like other Latin American countries, it was already beginning to adapt the new economic model. Various governments, among them those of Osvaldo Furtado and Leon Febres Cordero, took charge of the structural adjustments: the elimination of state controls on oil drilling and production, the signing of agreements with the International Monetary Fund, the elimination of bank regulations, the elimination of limits on foreign investments, the reduction of import tariff protection and the elimination of subsidies. Toward the year 1994, the economic reforms were deepened, and in particular, measures were taken with regard to the financial system. Exchange and interest rates were deregulated, a strict monetary policy was adopted, it was attempted to control inflation through exchange rates, and mini-devaluations were applied (Araujo Garcia: 2006).

Various factors of a political and economic nature, both national and international, converged in the Ecuadorian crisis at the end of the 90's, and attempting to blame the Isaias Group for it is nothing short of irresponsible.

Firstly, we should keep in mind that the globalization and internationalization processes in the economy, in addition to their advantages, brought with them the risk of the global effects of local and regional crises. Around mid-1998, Latin America was experiencing the effects of the Asian crisis that had originated in Thailand, and according to certain astute individuals, "...as in the case of the first crisis of its kind (the one in Mexico in 1994 and 1995), the Asian crisis was a result of the destabilizing effects of private international cash flow. It was a debt-deflation crisis" (Guillen R: 2000). The crisis obviously hit different countries in different ways. Mexico, for example, was able to rely on the support of the economic dynamics of its neighbor to the north in order to overcome the crisis. However, most countries suffered from a decreased growth rate. Colombia, the country with which Ecuador maintains a fluid economic exchange, is an example of the magnitude of the effects of the economic crisis experienced at that time. This country has been characterized by prudent economic management. It was the only country in Latin America that grew during the 80's, which economists refer to as the "lost decade." Colombia has not changed its currency, has no incidents of annual inflation higher than 32% in its modern economic history, and its growth rates have fluctuated between 3% and 5%. However, in 1999, it experienced its first economic recession since the crisis of '29, six decades earlier. In general, the effects spread throughout the region and, "in the face of uncertainty about the future of emerging markets, investors abandoned these countries, seeking refuge in the markets of developed countries."

Secondly, we must consider that Ecuador had internal problems, which made the development of the crisis inescapable. The country was coming out of a war with Peru, known as the Cenepa War, forcing it to allocate a large amount of resources to this cause, which had subsequent consequences on the acuteness of the financial crisis. Furthermore, between October of 1997 and August of 1998, Ecuador suffered the consequences of the El Niño phenomenon. This climatic condition dealt a hard blow to agricultural production. The resulting stagnation, in turn, led to the accumulation of past-due obligations in the financial system, and banks had problems with international lines of credit.

In 1998, the Ecuadorian economy demonstrated a 43.4% inflation rate, the highest in Latin America, recorded growth of barely 0.8% and ended the year with a 6% deficit in its Gross National Product (Zuniga: 2000).

Ecuador began to experience one of the most severe economic crises of its entire history. Its economic indicators were the worst ever. There was no confidence in the financial system, there was a recession in the production mechanism and there were zero foreign investments. The rapid increase in the debt portfolio, a byproduct of the depression of businesses for three consecutive years, combined with a fiscal crisis, drove the public to begin withdrawing money from the banks with the goal of sheltering it in dollars. This affected the private banking sector, which in turn led to the request for liquidity advances from the Central Bank (Cerdas et al: 2006).

The nearly twofold increase in the price of gasoline, basic provisions and electricity marked the beginning of the uncontrolled devaluation of the sucre, which was aggravated by freezing half of all bank deposits. Speculation on the dollar grew at an unsustainable rate and soon worsened what little solvency there was in the Ecuadorian financial system.

In Berchi's opinion, the previously mentioned economic measures by the government, which were intended to prevent a drop in international reserves and the hyperinflation that was already being glimpsed, had the following results, which reflected an absolute loss of confidence in the Ecuadorian financial system:

- There was a huge leak of capital, approximately 43% of all deposits, between January of 1998 and December of 1999
- The sucre was devaluated even more in relation to the dollar: in 1999, the exchange rate went from 7,114 sucres per dollar to 17,982. By the 10th of January of the year 2000, when the government announced plans for dollarization, the sucre had passed the barrier of 25,000 sucres per dollar and applied this conversion rate (Berchi et al: 2000).

Lastly, it is interesting to read the analysis of the 1999 crisis and the dollarization initiative by the economist Rafael Correa in an article published in La Insignia in July of 2004, where he attributes the blame for the crisis to the government for its poor financial controls, which were diametrically opposed to the President's demagogical and populist position, when he blamed the Isaias Group for the crisis and proceeded to seize all of its assets: "...the unilateral Ecuadorian dollarization was adopted in January of 2000 after the worst crisis in the country's history. Nevertheless, the crisis of 1998-1999 was essentially a bank crisis, the result of the financial deregulation of 1994 combined with inadequate controls, a weak banking system, poor financial practices and negative external clashes beginning in 1995. This bank crisis was transformed into a currency crisis as a direct consequence of the Law of the Deposit Guarantee Agency (the AGD Law), which obligated the State to insure 100% of national and foreign deposits with no limit as to their amount. As a byproduct of that, the Central Government created the AGD bonds and the Central Bank of Ecuador injected liquidity in order to acquire these bonds and guarantee the deposits. In this way, the 400% depreciation of the national currency between January of 1999 and January of 2000, as well as the threatening acceleration of monthly inflation, both justifications for adopting dollarization, would not have occurred if there had not been excess liquidity in the economy."

In conclusion, the dollarization of the Ecuadorian economy assumed by President Mahaud is a faithful reflection of the gravity and complexity of the crisis experienced in Ecuador, which could not have been caused by Filanbanco. Hyperinflation, economic instability and speculation, in turn, were reflected in the principle economic indicators: "...with regard to the macroeconomic indicators, the fiscal deficit, which was at -1.5% in relation to the GNP, increased to -5.8%. Nevertheless, the payment of interest on the public debt (internal and external) increased to 7% of the GNP. If we add the amortization of the public debt on top of the interest payments, the gross financing needs were almost 11.8% of the GNP in 1998 and 11% in 1999. Furthermore, the total public debt service (external and internal) of around 16 billion dollars approached 50% of all exports of non-factorial goods and services."

3
FILANBANCO: THE SUCCESS OF THE ISAIAS GROUP

Filanbanco was closed under the control of the Ecuadorian government in July of 2001, not under the control of the Isaias'

Virtue, dedication, sacrifice and austerity are the qualities that have characterized the majority of successful entrepreneurs and businessmen throughout the world. However, Emilio Isaias Abi Hanna needed much more than that in order to have built one of the strongest and most powerful financial empires in Ecuador from the ground up within a few decades. His work deserves high praise, and to date, has been continued by three subsequent generations of Isaias' with the same great care and determination that he invested in it from the very beginning.

The war forced millions of people to escape from its horrors, seeking refuge and redistributing themselves all over the world, but many countries benefited from their interactions with the new arrivals that brought their talents and cultures with them. Emilio Isaias, like thousands of Lebanese, fled from poverty and the Turkish draft during the Balkan War. He embarked on a voyage to Ecuador with the equivalent of a thousand dollars in his pocket at age 19, full of hopes and dreams. He could have come to any other country. Docking in an Ecuadorian port was pure chance and not a predetermined destiny. Likewise, with his vision and entrepreneurial spirit, he could have become rich and successful anywhere.

More surprising than Emilio Isaias' natural business instincts or his keen eye for good opportunities for growth was his determination to do business in any part of the world. At the beginning of 1927, he traveled to Great Britain to contract venders and bolster textile imports, which then formed the basis of his companies. He also took advantage of his three-month stay in the country to improve his English. With the economic crisis in full swing, in the year 1932, he sent his brother, Lutfallah, to Kobe, Japan to bring back silk and cashmere.

His exceptional capacity for creating companies enabled him to convert a personal tragedy into an opportunity for internationalizing his business. At the end of 1944, he suffered a hemorrhage and was diagnosed with colon cancer. He was successfully operated on in Rochester, United States and moved to New York, where he founded the "South and North Corporation," dedicated to the purchase of raw fabric made of viscose fiber, which was sent out for printing. He continued in textiles until he founded the San Vicente textile mill in 1947, which represented the most important textile industry of its kind in the country, with modern equipment and nearly 950 looms. In this way, he became the pioneer of textile modernization in Ecuador, applying the knowledge he acquired in countries that were at the cutting edge of the textile industry at that time, such as Great Britain and Japan.

In 1951, the family founded EICA, using the Spanish initials of the "Emilio Isaias Commercial Corporation," which was primarily dedicated to the import and commercialization of primary goods. Hard work and vision started to pay off and the group grew, and started to diversify, not only in the textile sector but obtained the representation for CASE, John Deere, and Evinrude. They also expanded in the agribusiness sector as well as other industrial and real estate investments. , not only in Ecuador but in New York and Miami, where they also acquired Republic National Bank of Miami, that became one of the largest Hispanic banks in Dade County.

Filanbanco, a small bank acquired during this expansion period of the group under the name of Caja de Ahoros la Filantropica was not the result of financial acrobatics or speculation. It came about through diversification and specially focused in supporting the growing commercial and agricultural businesses basically in the coastal zone of Ecuador. Later it became to have a role as the bank for the agricultural, aquaculture and industrial sectors in Ecuador.

FILANBANCO UNDER THE ISAIAS GROUP'S CONTROL

In 1958, the Isaias Group, headed by Pedro, made one of its best investments, which paradoxically became a headache four decades later for Roberto and William Isaias, thanks to the fierce political persecution by the Government and the envy and pettiness of the media and certain entrepreneurs who could not tolerate the success of others.

The Group acquired La Filantropica Savings, which was undergoing financial difficulties at the time. Pedro did not manage the entity for long, as he died in 1960. However, during his short time at the head of the institution, he initiated the Group's financial consolidation, especially in the industrial sector. Under his management, the Group founded a bottling plant for distributing Canada Dry soft drinks, and at the same time, another of his brothers, Estefano, also contributed to the Group's diversification through numerous dealerships, most importantly in tractors and outboard motors. The confidence of foreign investors in the Group also facilitated its growth, given its solidity and its businesses in New York and Miami.

Upon the accidental death of Pedro, direction of the La Filantropica Bank was assumed by Enrique Emilio. New contributions, new investments and increased growth were not halted by the criminal act that took Enrique's life in January of 1965.

Once again, another Isaias emerged on the business scene. In spite of his youth, Nahim took over the administration of the bank, and this same year, the Group also benefited from the young, fresh contributions of Roberto, William and Emilio, who had recently graduated in the United States, and now fully dedicated themselves to the family business. Roberto focused on the commercial sector in Guayaquil, the main headquarters for the import, commercialization and distribution of the textiles manufactured by the Group. William and Emilio focused on textile production in Quito. Upon the arrival of Estefano, Roberto's younger brother, administrative functions were redistributed. Roberto took over the bank's financial activities and Estefano dedicated himself to textile distribution. At that time, there were four third-generation Isaias', young Ecuadorians, trained abroad and fully committed to the family business, modernizing everything, applying cutting-edge technologies and also learning from the experience and business instincts of their parents and uncles.

Early on, in 1965, the Isaias Group began automating the bank. It was the first bank in Ecuador to leave semi-manual operations behind. At that time, transaction records were kept in books, using pen and ink. Nahim imported NCR technology that was starting to be used to modernize the banking services throughout the world.

Roberto recounts how the bank grew and became automated: "The bank was the first to start automation because of its growth through a more friendly approach to its clients, without that image of banks as temples of money where one must enter with great reverence. Our bank was completely open, up close and personal. People could come in and talk to the manager, tell him their problems and ask for credit frankly. You could say that it was a bank with open doors. People felt calm and confident there. Most of our clientele consisted of people with a little nest egg, people with small companies or family businesses, farmers from the coast and merchants. Since we had been in commerce, many of the merchants knew my grandfather, my uncles and my father very well and trusted them, which made it much easier to do business with them. This caused the bank to advance very quickly and it just grew and grew."

In 1978, La Filantropica became Filanbanco. At that time, it was one of the most solid banks in

Ecuador, and a few years later, it became the country's premier bank. However, it was not only the application of technology and modernization that positioned the bank. There were two fundamental elements. One was what some today call "personalized attention," which Filanbanco was already practicing in the 80's. The other was the establishment of lines of credit for foreign commerce. In a region dedicated to agriculture and shrimp production for export, it was crucial to have these lines of credit. Roberto notes: "We had huge lines of credit with foreign banks that had a lot of trust in Filanbanco, and we extended these credit facilities to our clients in the commercial, industrial, export and import sectors all over Ecuador. This was fundamental to Ecuador's international commerce throughout this period."

In the mid 90's, Filanbanco managed approximately 50% of Ecuador's international business, and its lines of credit reached 700 million dollars, which was more than the rest of the country's banks combined could offer. "The bank's ability to contribute to national projects and its backup capital, which was the highest in the country," says Roberto Isaias, "consolidated us as the largest bank among strong competitors, which at that time were Banco del Pichincha in the Andean area and Banco del Pacifico on the coast. The vast majority of credit lines were extended in the coast, especially in Guayaquil, were practically all agribusiness credit was extended through Filanbanco and Pacifico because Pichincha was in the mountains, where farmers weren't focused on exports, as they were more interested in internal commerce in the area. Headquartered in Guayaquil the country's largest commercial city in Ecuador, these two banks were dedicated to extending credit to the agricultural sectors, for the aquaculture for export and commercial credit facilities. In an interview granted by Roberto to Ramon Jimeno (Jimeno 2006: 138), he goes on to say: "I think that Filanbanco had a significant role in Ecuador's agricultural growth and I believe that we were responsible for the growth of the country's shrimp industry. We extended probably more than 50 or 60 percent of our credit to people who were involved in the shrimp industry, especially shrimp farming. We were extremely active in that field. We were also the source of financial support for the growth of the country's banana and cacao industries. In general, I would say that we were responsible for a large percentage of the agricultural growth on the coast of Ecuador."

Roberto adds, "Of course, besides supporting the agricultural and shrimp sectors, we supported all commerce, all imports, and provided long-term financing for many industries. I believe that we did a magnificent job in helping many clients to grow, passing from, I would say, mid-level to a much higher level. The people of the Ecuadorian coast are normally self-starters and aggressive businessmen, who love to open new frontiers and new businesses, which is exactly what they did with bananas and shrimp, becoming, at that time, the world's largest exporters of both products. And they were able to do it because they could count on the support of Filanbanco. That's why we were important."

Roberto also speaks of Filanbanco's image before the crisis: "Well, there were studies, surveys and group sessions, all of which are normally done in order to orient advertising, and the consistent result was that people had a very good image of the bank, which I think was a natural response to the bank's attitude towards them. That is, I think that this positive image was also a fundamental component of that situation that allowed us to become the size we became, and also because of that, we became the country's premier bank. If we hadn't had that positive image, I don't believe that we could have been the country's premier bank. People trusted us very much. They not only trusted Filanbanco, but also the Isaias name. People had great respect for our family and felt supported by the Isaias' that stood behind the bank, thanks to our family's history and its behavior, which we sustained during all those decades through three generations. People could trust the bank because Filanbanco was the only financial institution at that time that had such substantial capital, a little over a hundred and fifty million dollars."

THE CRISIS

By the mid 90's, the Ecuadorian financial system was already showing deep fissures. In 1996, the State intervened in a bank in Quito to prevent its closure. Between the middle of '96 and '97, the El Niño phenomenon dealt a blow to agriculture and this had a devastating effect on Filanbanco, which had the majority of its portfolio in this sector and which, furthermore, managed 40 percent of the country's private foreign commerce and 20 percent of its banking business. So, the international crisis began to be felt in Ecuador, as it motivated restrictions on foreign lines of credit. International banks not only restricted lines of credit for financing new operations, but also did not renew existing credit facilities, causing a significant egress of the bank's liquid assets in payment of such credits.

People could not pay their credit obligations. The bank proceeded to refinance the debt, and by June 30th of 1998, had achieved a 30 million dollar increase in capital. However, this was not enough, as President Jamil Mahaud contributed to the creation of an economic panic with his imprudent statements about the country's financial situation. At the end of one of his cabinet meetings, after less than a month of being hounded by journalists, he stated that the country was a sinking Titanic, and that they were studying the problem of the financial system and its insolvency, mentioning Filanbanco as one of the problem banks.

These statements from the mouth of a President of the Republic on their own were enough to create an economic panic in any country of the world, even in the absence of national or international economic crises. However, the worst part of all was that the government did not implement a single measure that would restore confidence to accountholders and, instead, produced the opposite effect when it passed a law to control the situation, in which it levied a tax on the transfer of capital, which was nothing more than a tax on banking transactions.

In light of the President's words and the measures that were taken, accountholders had no other alternative except to withdraw all of their funds from the banking system as quickly as possible, which is exactly what they did. The massive withdrawals not only affected Filanbanco, which was the country's largest bank with more than a million customers, but also spread the crisis in the financial system to 22 additional banks, among them small banks like Solbanco in Guayaquil and medium-sized banks like Prestamos in Quito.

Obviously, the withdrawals from Filanbanco mounted with dizzying speed. By mid-September, the bank had to turn to the Central Bank's liquidity loans, in accordance with the regulations of that time. The legislation that was in effect in that area allowed the bank to withdraw a certain percentage of its capital, collateralizing 140 percent of the loan through its portfolio qualified as "A" by the Central Bank. Between September 14th and December 2nd, Filanbanco effectuated withdrawals in sucres in the equivalent of 420 million dollars and paid an additional 80 million dollars in interest charged in advance and other financial fees, that is, a scandalous interest rate of nearly 500 percent, which represented more than a million dollars per day.

As it was impossible for Filanbanco to obtain more funding from the Central Bank, it was proposed that the government take over the bank or else allow it to be liquidated voluntarily. Since the government knew the impact that the latter option would have on what was left of a financial system already turned on its head, it opted to take possession of the bank on December 2nd of 1998, for which purposes, the government managed to persuade Congress to approve the creation of the

Deposit Guarantee Agency (AGD), which permitted it to take over financial institutions with problems at that time and in the future.

FILANBANCO UNDER THE STATE'S CONTROL

In practice, the government's intervention in Filanbanco began with management of the bank's line of credit resources. The Central Bank of Ecuador, in compliance with the law, partially disbursed the loaned funds, in accordance with the cash flow necessities of the bank's treasury; these were used to directly pay banks and international institutions, to directly cover the needs of the Clearing House for covering checks issued by clients to make deposits in other local banks, and a small portion was credited to the bank so that it could attend to the cash withdrawals of its accountholders who turned to the teller windows to withdraw their savings deposits, all of this under strict control and daily balance audits.

This is why the Manager of the Central Bank of Ecuador (BCE) not only told the Attorney General that there had never been any misuse of funds on the part of Filanbanco when it was administered by members of the Isaias family and that the previously mentioned loans had been paid in full, but also submitted proof that they had always exercised control and monitoring of those resources. With this irrefutable evidence, the Chief Justice of the Supreme Court at that time, admitting the Attorney General's ruling, dismissed the charges against the BCE officials who had been investigated for granting and transacting loans, but did not issue the same ruling for the Isaias brothers. Although it seems like a lie, the same evidence served to exonerate some parties but not others. This can only be understood within the framework of the political persecution unleashed from that point on against the Group.

On the transparent management given to the liquidity funds granted to Filanbanco up to December 2nd of 1998, which was the day the government took over the bank, in "The guilt of the innocent," Ramon Jimeno says the following: "...The use given to the funds obtained by Filanbanco through the liquidity loans authorized by the Central Bank of Ecuador is substantiated, according to the defense lawyers, by the report of the experts designated by the Supreme Court of Justice and the Report on Sources and Uses from the Central Bank of Ecuador, in which it was determined that there was no misuse of the Central Bank's resources and, furthermore, that these resources were insufficient to meet the bank's liquidity requirements, for which reason Filanbanco used its own resources stemming from the recovery of its credit portfolio. This is verified by the General Manager of Filanbanco designated by the Deposit Guarantee Agency, Engineer Antonio Bejarano Trujillo, who, in an official communiqué of December 5th of 2000 (Communiqué No. 200-443-GG) fully details the correct use of the funds."

"Furthermore, in the case file, there is a report by Elvira Pino and Fernando Castillo, the experts designated by the Ninth Judge of the Pichincha Penal Court, which commissioned the report, in which it is clearly established that the Central Bank monitored and supervised the correct use of the funds by the private administrators of Filanbanco between September 14th December 2nd of 1998."

"The presumed increase in Filanbanco's portfolio balances, cited in the reports that led to the Formal Audit, were invalidated in the proceedings by the presence of the document, "Overall analysis of the portfolio report," originating from the Central Bank of Ecuador, regarding Filanbanco and Filanbanco Trust, from which it was determined that not only there was no increase in portfolio levels during the term of the Central Bank's liquidity loans, but that, on the contrary, Filanbanco recovered 25,992,000 dollars. It is also recorded in the proceedings that, during the period in which Filanbanco was assisted by credit from the Central Bank, its Various Investments account decreased from 137 million dollars to 7 million dollars, thus discrediting any allegations of its growth, as claimed in the reports of the Superintendence of Banks, which led to the Formal Audit. It is recorded that the statements contained in the Formal Audit to the effect that the Various Investments Account grew by 13,000,000 dollars and 35,000,000 dollars on October 30th and December 2nd of 1998, respectively, had been proven to be false by the cited Statement of Sources and Uses from the Central Bank of Ecuador, by the report of the experts, Fernando Castillo and Elvira Pino, and by the engineer, Antonio Bejarano Trujillo, the Manager of Filanbanco appointed by the AGD."

"From these reports, it is determined that, on October 30th of 1998, the Central Bank delivered the sum of 8,700,961 dollars and that, on that same date, Filanbanco paid the sum of 5,948,710 dollars in interest only and an additional 4,086,551 dollars for operating expenses, for which the funds from that day were insufficient, making it necessary for Filanbanco to use its own funds to effectuate the payments. It is also shown that, on December 2nd of 1998, Filanbanco received 8,853,610 dollars from the Central Bank of Ecuador, which was allocated to address liquidity requirements and, as such, it is impossible to have allocated those funds for another purpose, as alleged in the Superintendence of Banks' report."

"By December 2nd of 1998, the day on which Filanbanco was turned over to the AGD by its original owners, the liquidity credit granted to Filanbanco by the Central Bank of Ecuador had risen to 423 million dollars. The records in the proceedings include the certification issued by the Central Bank stating that the private administration of Filanbanco paid this credit in full, both principle and interest, and show that this interest amounted to 1,000,000 dollars per day for Filanbanco, an interest rate that surpassed 500% APR."

Under the administration of the Deposit Guarantee Agency, Filanbanco initiated a quick financial recovery process, thanks to the perception of security and confidence that the Ecuadorian State's guarantee gave to old and new clients. According to a report from ING Barings, an advisory firm contracted to supervise and restructure the bank before it's sale, six months after being turned over to the government, Filanbanco had bolstered its deposits, had assets equal to the balance shown at the time it was turned over, had generated a hundred million dollars in profits and was ready to be returned to private ownership. ING's advice was that the bank should be sold at that exact moment, as there were international financial institutions interested in acquiring it. Furthermore, this had been the government's initial proposal.

However, the government changed its plans. First, they said because of the bank's performance. The rumors of insolvency had disappeared, there were sufficient funds to back up any transaction and Filanbanco continued to be an efficient, modern and solid bank, recovering its position as the premier bank in Ecuador. Secondly, because under the new law that created the AGD, Central Bank was not allowed to extend liquidity loans creating new difficulties to banks in need, having nowhere to turn in the event of an emergency, as the crisis in the Ecuadorian financial system had not been completely overcome.

Under these circumstances, the monetary and banking authorities found a solution to the prohibition on those loans by converting Filanbanco into a "bank of banks," a mechanism for saving certain institutions that the State was interested in saving. The bank was forced to grant loans and receive portfolio and/or shares of banks with problems and to receive Certificates of Restructuring (CDR's) issued by other banks for amounts that were far beyond its capacity. This bank salvation process between August of 1999 and May of 2000 included 63 million dollars in loans to Banco Pacifico, 49.6 million to Banco Popular, 2.5 million to Cofiec, and another 67 million to Banco La Previsora, among other institutions.

This was the beginning of the poor administration and corrupt management of Filanbanco under the State administration. At the end of 1999, with the goal of saving Banco La Previsora from insolvency, due to its serious problems making it impossible for the bank to stay afloat, the financial authorities forced Filanbanco to enter into a merger by absorption agreement with La Previsora, an institution to which, additionally, more than a hundred million dollars had been advanced. At the beginning of the year 2000, the Superintendence of Banks approved the definitive merger of the two banks. This forced Filanbanco to assume Previsora's and Previsora Internacional's significant liabilities and the exaggerated severance pay of its employees, to each of whom it paid seven years of salary, obligations that represented approximately 70 million dollars. The majority of the employees, who had already received this compensation, were rehired by the merged bank, creating an additional burden on the bank's already high operating costs. These type of transactions began to mark Filanbanco's progressive and definitive decline.

With Falconi Puig presiding over the AGD in his position as Superintendent of Banks, the greatest outrages were committed. As Roberto Isaias says, "...he is the key figure in those decisions that were made to decapitalize Filanbanco in order to save other banks. That is, the crises in other banks sustained the anxiety in the market; the people became distrustful and started filing claims for their money to be returned. That is when the AGD issued its famous reprogrammable certificates, delivered them to the people and found nothing better to do than to force Filanbanco to redeem them, converting them into Filanbanco's portfolio. These certificates were traded in the market at a 40% or 50% discount, but the AGD decided that Filanbanco should redeem them at face value, a crazy idea, to put it nicely."

"Filanbanco was doing nothing more than exchanging its cash funds for these pieces of paper from the AGD. Filanbanco received these papers, these certificates, in payment of obligations totaling 120 million dollars within a very short time, which did tremendous harm to its situation, as these papers had that huge discount. So, all of the bank's liquidity, which in June had been perfectly good, began to deteriorate at the end of '99, and in the year 2000, Filanbanco went into a crisis where it lost nearly 100 million dollars. That is, from profits of 140 million dollars that the bank had recorded when it was being advised by ING, the institution that recommended that the State should sell it; by the end of the year 2000, the bank administered under the AGD had lost nearly 100 million dollars. Then in 2001,

Filanbanco lost another 90 million dollars just before its closure."

The Directors of the AGD and their horrible decisions contributed to the bank's insolvency, and even after its closure, they continued to maintain chauffeurs, bodyguards and numerous other personnel that were no longer necessary, and that, furthermore, had been increased when Filanbanco was turned over to the State. From any point of view, this staff was excessive for an institution that was no longer active. Roberto Isaias continues, "...unbelievable things happened, it was the *vox populi*, as the clients' documents were sold for 10 percent of their value and properties owned by the bank were sold for 20 percent of their purchase price. Let's just say that they were having a field day with the bank and certain people were getting rich thanks to the situation in Filanbanco."

In April of 2001, the administration of Filanbanco passed from the AGD to the Ministry of Finances, and in July of that same year, the bank closed its doors with an announcement that it would reopen three days later, when it would be able to apply what was called "a market solution." However, that never happened. Miguel Davila, who was the head of the Banking Superintendence and whose duty was to close Filanbanco, in an interview granted to Ramon Jimeno (Jimeno

2006:110), expressed the following with regard to the principle causes for the definitive closure of the bank, first under the control of its shareholders and then under State control: "There was a generalized crisis in the Ecuadorian economy, poor fiscal management, a poor business environment, the El Niño phenomenon and, no doubt, I would say, insufficient capitalization of the entire financial system. There was not an adequate response on the part of either the authorities or the financial system, considering the enormous size of the problems we were facing. And obviously, during the crisis, it was very poor political management to approve the AGD Law in the terms in which it was approved." With regard to the bank when it was under State control, he says: "...If by that I am referring to the causes up to December 2nd of '98, when the bank went into public hands, from then on, the reason for the closure of Filanbanco was, without a doubt, the poor administration, the worst possible administration of Filanbanco on the part of the State, and a series of irregularities, many of which are now being tried or are just coming to light. I hope that even more will come to light in the future, as I said in my report, a comprehensive report, where the losses during the bank's administration by the State were determined to be 814 million dollars through seven different mechanisms. It is obvious that the State, itself, poorly administered the bank's resources with the result that the only possible decision, the only viable decision was to close the entity, in spite of the social and economic costs that might entail."

4

THE ORIGINS OF A TREACHEROUS AND RUTHLESS VENDETTA

The Superintendent of Banks invented a crime that did not previously exist in Ecuadorian law

Juan Falconi Puig, who presided over the AGD as the Superintendent of Banks, and who caused the fall of Filanbanco with his poor and suspicious measures while the bank was under government control, requested the Attorney General in June of 2000 –one month before the bank's closure – to investigate and then file charges against Roberto and William Isaias for the crime of "bank embezzlement." This crime did not even exist in the Ecuadorian Penal Code until May of 1999, and we must not forget that Filanbanco was turned over to the State on December 2nd of 1998.

Why was this Superintendent of Banks the originator of a personal and political vendetta that later snowballed, involving prosecutors, judges, Chief Justices of the Supreme Court, Presidents of the Republic and the media?

In many of the world's countries, it is very common to observe that businessmen and the most powerful economic class are closely linked to political activities. In the majority of cases where the states do not have independent and autonomous institutional structures, this results in illegal benefits or acts that are simply corrupt. However, this is not the case with the Isaias Group in Ecuador. The growth of this group was not due to privileges granted by the State, nor to privileges granted by the political class, but rather to the hard, pioneering work of its founding grandfather, work which was continued for three subsequent generations.

Among its family members, the Isaias family hasn't had Presidents, Vice-Presidents, Ministers or other powerful members of the official bureaucracy, who could have used their influence to obtain political or financial measures in the Group's favor. The Group has not organized political movements for purposes of gaining privileges by this route, either. Outside of the short political stint of Pedro as the representative of the province of Galapagos in the National Congress and that of Alfredo, who took his place in Congress after his accidental death, only Roberto Isaias briefly participated in the government of Abdala Bucaram as a financial advisor, which lasted no more than three months and did not entail any executive or directorial responsibilities. This appointment was the fruit of a long friendship forged through the economic activities that the two families carried out in Guayaquil.

So, Falconi's old hatred did not stem from any political practices of the Isaias family, but instead from the fair and square loss of an economic opportunity to the Isaias Group. What generated the initial hatred of the Superintendent against the Isaias Group, and specifically against Roberto, was the impossibility for Falconi to hang on to the Aztra Sugar Mill.

The history of Azucarera Tropical Americana S.A. (AZTRA), which is now called La Troncal Sugar Mill, enabled the rise of a town by the same name, which gained height in the 70's. At the hands of the State and under the military dictatorship, occurred what Ecuadorians remember as "The October 18th Massacre" or the "Aztra Massacre." The refinery workers had declared a strike, which was overly prolonged by the belligerence of the parties and which led to the death of several employees. Eyewitnesses and members of the syndicate who experienced the events recall that there were about 120 victims, the result of military oppression against a peaceful demonstration in which workers were simply defending their labor rights. From that point on, the company faced a series of legal and political problems that continued throughout the 80's and the 90's, which discouraged investors' interest in the company in which the State held 98% of the shares through the National Financial Corporation (CFN).

Roberto describes the initial relationship between the Isaias' and the Aztra Sugar Mill as follows: "This is a sugar mill that, around the year 1965, belonged to the Andrade Ochoa Group and was headed by Andrade, the engineer who built it using French financing. Its shareholders included the equipment manufacturers, the Filille, who owned 20 percent of the shares, a large group of the region's sugarcane farmers, and the Andrade Ochoa family, which was in charge of the plant. It so happened that Aztra could not pay its debt to the French, which was 17 million dollars at that time, so the family came to speak to us, because we, our family, had the necessary financial capacity and we also had a very small sugar mill, which fostered a certain relationship between us because we were in the same business. They proposed, 'Why doesn't your family capitalize the Sugar Mill?' So we said okay." (Jimeno 2006:180)

"At that time," Roberto continues, "we capitalized Aztra with something like one million, three hundred thousand dollars. Later, in the year '72, the military coup occurred, in which President Velasco Ibarra was removed from office during his final term. The French had the agreement and there was a necessity for long-term refinancing of the entire 17 million dollars, but the people administering the refinery put it off and didn't do it.

This was while we were contributing our money, so we put ourselves in charge. What happened next was that the military wanted to purchase several Mirage planes from France and the Fililles, the French creditors, saw an opportunity to make a proposal to the government: 'Gentlemen, there is this outstanding debt; take care of it because the French government won't be able to finance the planes if this situation isn't resolved.' Then the government entity, the National Financial Corporation, called us saying, 'Gentlemen, you have to sell the Sugar Mill to us.'"

"So, we had to sell it to them, and in that way, we managed to recoup our investment, but nothing more, not a penny more. They paid us exactly what we had invested and the CFN took over the Sugar Mill in the year '72. They started a very good management at first, but later they used it for their political interests. Instead of having 1,500 employees, the Aztra had 4,000, because they made it part of that policy of providing work for those who voted for a certain party and such things. So, with this extra burden, both the amount of workers and their limited abilities, as the goal was to provide employment, but not necessarily to those who were prepared to do the work, the Aztra Sugar Mill began to report significant losses. Thus came about the reign of Mr. Falconi, and any analyst could tell you, in spite of what the books say (because Falconi ordered things like eliminating the existing debt with the French from the books, although it had never been paid off), that during this time the sugar mill lost 8, 10 and 15 million dollars and had become a bottomless pit for the National Financial Corporation, which was supporting it. This sugar mill cost the National Financial Corporation a huge amount of money. And as if that weren't enough, the chaos of managing all of the personnel turned into a big labor problem. So, the decision was made to close the sugar mill." (Jimeno 2006:181)

In February of 1994, the National Financial Corporation issued a prospectus for the sale of Aztra's shares, which also contained the company's financial statements, prepared by Price Waterhouse. There were no takers except for the Isaias Group, so the CFN sold the shares in Aztra for 100,000 dollars to its creditor, who would have to assume more than a hundred million dollars in liabilities, all of which have been paid in full and on time. Much earlier, the company Global Trade Financing Corp. had demanded payment of Aztra's debts in the Fourth Chamber of the Supreme Court of Justice, but this was prior to the sales process. On the basis of the confession of Hector Apolo Cuenca, the ex-manager of Aztra, the Fourth Chamber of the Guayaquil Superior Court acknowledged the company's debt.

The manager of the National Financial Corporation at the time, Leonardo Stagg, responded to certain criticism that had been raised about the legality of the sale of the CFN's shares in the Aztra Sugar Mill. He indicated, "...It was evident that the CFN's shares in Aztra were worthless and that the Corporation needed to transfer those shares in order to reactivate the company, a task that was assumed by the buyers in order to defend the employment positions, to provide a basic necessity like sugar, to boost the economy of a forgotten region of the country and to safeguard the creditors. These important objectives explain the way in which the CFN proceeded in this matter of notorious complexity." Stagg also added that in 1974, the CFN acquired 81% of the shares in Aztra through a government mandate of that time. "It was not about capitalizing credits, but rather a transaction intended to prevent the sugar mill from becoming paralyzed and to find a viable way to settle the French debt stemming from the provision of equipment." Lastly, Stagg confirms that both the labor problem faced by the company and its accumulated debt accelerated the losses, which is why the CFN's shares in Aztra were offered for sale through the stock market.

Falconi, who was interested in purchasing Aztra, lost this first match with us, says Roberto Isaias. However, he did not accept his defeat with dignity. As the Minister of Industry, at that time, he stated that the debts contracted with the Isaias' would not be paid and that the lawsuit would be successful. Later, the Minister of Industry filed a new lawsuit against the Isaias Group for the use of the Biela brand name in a brewery that was constructed by them. The lawsuit did not last long, but the resentment of the Minister of Industry against the Group did.

After Falconi charged Roberto and William with "bank embezzlement," in order to cover up the mismanagement of the AGD and the Superintendence of Banks, he initiated a systematic hate campaign against the Group, through the radio, newspapers and television, influencing public opinion by making the Isaias' appear to be responsible for the insolvency of Filanbanco and the economic crisis in Ecuador.

The misdeeds of the Superintendent were recorded as follows by Ramon Jimeno in "The guilt of the innocent:" "The third phase of the administration of Filanbanco on the part of the State began at the end of the year 1999 and ended with the suspension of operations in July of the year 2001 and the subsequent liquidation process, which happened a year later. At this stage, the balance sheets, the reports by the Superintendence of Banks, itself, and those by the international advisors, as well as the opinions of the auditing firms, all of which are incorporated into evidence, reveal that there was a notable decline between April and December of the year 2000. Filanbanco lost its liquidity and its solvency."

"The search for the reasons behind this situation has shed light on the following: the first of these was the deficient and unprofessional administration of the bank, which the auditors qualify as an absence of management in the administration of its assets; the second was Executive Decree No. 1492 of November 10th of 1999, which forced financial institutions to redeem Reprogrammed Certificates of Deposit (CDR's) at face value, solely in order to pay the debts of their clients, up to the National Financial Corporation's debt limit, which in the case of Filanbanco, was about 64 million dollars at that time."

"What was the bearing of this legal provision? Its bearing depends on the extent to which it is applied: the State administrators of Filanbanco decided to exceed this 64 million dollar limit, and furthermore, not only redeemed those CDR's to pay the stated debts, but also had Filanbanco pay them in cash, with no discount, which dramatically threatened the bank's liquidity and, due to the loss of value in its assets, it's net worth."

"On December 12th of 2000, an internal audit report on Filanbanco revealed that, between April 22nd of 1999 and October 13th of 2000, 183.9 million dollars had been negotiated in CDR's, including cash purchases at 100 percent of their face value. Various sources of information provide suspicious indications of "unconventional" management, for example, that between November 26th and December 2nd of 1999, Filanbanco paid the company Plainbridge, Inc., which had family ties to the Superintendent of Banks at that time, 100 percent of the face value in cash for CDR's amounting to 1,009,510.42 U.S. dollars, issued by Banco del Progreso, which was closed and in the process of reorganization."

"However, the mismanagement was not limited to a few specific actions. As shown in the evidence, in the year 2000, international advisors expressed their concerns about the State officials signing a document on October 4th of 1999, proposing a merger between Filanbanco and Banco La Previsora. In February of 2000, McKinsey Company, Inc., a consulting company hired to assist with the merger, indicated in its report that there was a high level of outstanding debt in the portfolio, as well as an inability on the part of the current agents to manage the portfolio's deterioration."

"This concern was shared even within the Superintendence of Banks, where a memorandum of February 18th of 2000, to the attention of the Superintendent, Dr. Juan Falconi Puig, indicated the financial problems of a structural nature that the merged entity would face. However, the Superintendent, ignoring the arguments expressed in those statements, would order the merger anyway, which for Filanbanco, implied a greater loss of its liquidity and a requirement for additional provisions, due to the poor quality of Banco La Previsora's assets."

"A report from Filanbanco's Treasury, dated June 28th of 2000, revealed that the bank would suffer a loss of 124 million dollars as a result of this merger with La Previsora, while there was also knowledge of a technical report by the Superintendence of Banks observing that the liquidity weaknesses would be accentuated with the merger, at the same time as the quality of the assets would deteriorate, both situations affecting the solvency of the merged bank. However, on the same day of this report, in an extraordinary session of the Banking Board, it was resolved to merge the two entities, and in another extraordinary session on August 31st, it was resolved to establish a trust in the name of the ex-shareholders of Banco La Previsora."

In another passage from the same book, Jimeno (Jimeno 2006:66) compiles other examples of the suspicious decisions made by the Superintendent of Banks in April of 2000 without first sending them to Congress for a vote: "On the 7th of that month, in a meeting of the merger committee for the banks Pacifico and Continental, it was resolved to officially support Banco del Pacifico, acknowledging that there were losses in this bank that no legal representative of the bank wanted to, or should, assume, due to the political and legal scandal it would cause. The redemption of CDR's at Pacifico created considerable losses in its net worth, while rumors circulated that the bank's real estate was oversized."

"On May 10th, Falconi Puig appeared before the Central Bank with the charges that led to the modification of the composition of that bank's Board of Directors, replacing it with a group made up of officials linked to Banco del Pacifico, an action that would become known to the public as the takeover of Central by 'the Pacifico Cartel.' On May 25th, it was decided to capitalize Banco del Pacifico with 89 million dollars, and six days later, the AGD's Board of Directors, with Falconi Puig presiding, approved this capitalization."

"On June 19th, based on the allegations in audit reports from the Superintendence of Banks of Guayaquil and Quito, prepared during the months of April and May of the year 2000, the Superintendence of Banks requested to the Chief Prosecutor of the Nation the initiation of a formal criminal investigation of an alleged offense of the former private administrators of Filanbanco. It is not a stretch to interpret this as a means of distracting attention away from the cases of Pacifico and Cofiec, a bank with close family ties to the Superintendent, which on the past 26th of April was unable to cover the liquidity credit granted to it by the Central Bank. These reports, which gave rise to the formal criminal investigation did not contain any concrete accusations of any crime, a circumstance that is clearly related to the fact that, until December of 1998, when Filanbanco was turned over to the State, the Superintendence of Banks had never imposed any penalties on the bank's administrators or shareholders for any type of irregularity, either administrative or criminal, related to the allegations in these reports that had formed the grounds for the formal criminal investigation."

"The corruption reached such an extent during the State's administration of Filanbanco that Miguel Davila, the new Superintendent of Banks, through a report requested from the Superintendence's technicians, discovered that the bank lost at least 814 million dollars during the period in which it was managed by the State." (Jimeno 2006)

Falconi was charged by the Office of the Chief Prosecutor on October 4th of 2001 for authorizing the merger of Filanbanco with Banco La Previsora S.A., causing public funds to be diverted in order to save a private bank, in detriment to Filanbanco, which was now a State bank. The Superintendent of Banks, displaying his uncanny ability to turn every situation where he was accused into an opportunity to become the accuser, responded by charging the Chief Prosecutor and the former Chief Justice of the Supreme Court with breach of public duty. Finally, the Superintendent was called to trial and removed from office by the National Congress in November of the same year.

Falconi was skillfully and artfully converting his personal vendetta into the State's political vendetta. He used his political relations and the influence that he still had in legal circles to cover up his dealings and to increase prejudice against the Isaias' among judges, Justices and influential politicians in order to condemn the entrepreneurs before they were even tried. Furthermore, the majority of the media became a sounding board for disseminating the notion that the closure of Filanbanco and Ecuador's economic crisis were not caused by the corruption of those who managed the bank, nor were they a result of the incompetence and erratic measures of the government to avert the crisis, but instead were exclusively the fault of the Isaias'. That was the slogan and it has been repeated for a decade now, impeding any possibility of a trial in accordance with the law.

As a consequence of this, the basest passions and fiercest sentiments against the Group's companies flourished among competing entrepreneurs. There was not nor has there been solidarity with the Isaias'. The Group's success from generation to generation has only caused envy on the part of certain less capable entrepreneurs, segments of the population infected by the discourse on the guilt of the Isaias' and political circles, which politicized justice in order to hinder a fair and transparent trial.

PERSECUTION IN THE COURTS

The judges and prosecutors that wanted to guarantee due process, defying the State organizations' predetermined guilty verdict in the case, were persecuted or dismissed. Roberto Isaias explains how the perversity of Falconi and the judges had no limits when it came to making accusations. Falconi accused Roberto and William of making "self-loans" and left people with the impression that a serious crime had been committed. Self-loans or loans to affiliates were not prohibited by law at that time, so they did not constitute any type of crime. Roberto explains: "...according to the law, at that time, banks could make loans to companies linked to their shareholders or their own investment structure up to the amount of patrimony. We were completely within the law, as we were below this limit. But he appeared and accused us, saying that we had made self-loans, without ever clarifying whether or not we were within regulations, leading people to believe that we weren't, that we had committed a crime. He never accused us of doing anything illegal; he accused us of 'having made self-loans.' And people assumed that we had committed a crime, a disgrace. Do you see the game he was playing?"

Roberto continues explaining what happened with that accusation: "The prosecution took this charge, began to process it and sent it to the judge. And the judge thus initiated an investigation, just like that, without fulfilling even the minimal requirements, which consisted of first appointing experts to see if the action was appropriate, if it was true or not that State funds had been used illegally. He didn't do it. He ignored the law in his proceedings and ordered our preventive custody and of other officials of the Central Bank, the Superintendence of Banks, the Banking Board and an endless number of government entities that had had some relation to the case. Subsequently, some of these people were released, including members of the Banking Board, officials of the Superintendence and even some of the auditors that had prepared the report stating that the loans were made legally, which was the strangest part of all. If we had misused funds, as he said, why release the auditors that had concluded in their audit that everything we had done was fine?"

The President of the Supreme Court, Roberto claims, requested that the Superintendent specify exactly what the accusations were, because up to that time, everything was supposition. Falconi requested a 15-day timeframe, at the end of which, no proof was submitted. Nevertheless, with no concrete accusations, the trial moved forward. The case of the Isaias brothers has been so politicized that no judge is willing to lift the order for preventive custody for fear of causing a scandal that would lead to dismissal or resignation.

In a desperate search for a concrete accusation, the President of the Supreme Court at that time turned the case over to the Chief Prosecutor of the Nation, Mariana Yepez, to proceed with the investigation and make her ruling. One of the critical points of the investigation, the key evidence or the axis on which the whole concept of "bank embezzlement" turns, was determining whether the funds granted by the Central Bank had been used appropriately or not.

As part of the investigation set in motion by the Chief Prosecutor, the General Manager of the Central Bank, in Official Communiqué SE-1462-200, informed Dr. Yepez that, in the presence of countless press reports on the use of the funds granted by the Central Bank of Ecuador to Filanbanco at the end of 1998, it was his duty to reveal to her the information related to these transactions and the corresponding financial analysis that the case required, with the goal of confirming the transparency with which the Central Bank of Ecuador had always operated. The conclusion that the Manager of the Central Bank made known in his communiqué to the Chief Prosecutor was the following: *"From the detailed explanation that is recorded in the present report, Mrs. Attorney General, on the results of the monitoring of Filanbanco performed by the Central Bank during the indicated period in which it accessed the Central Bank's lines of liquidity credit, both through tracking of the treasury and tracking of liquidity at the balance level, it can be inferred from the information provided by Filanbanco that the liquidity needs of said institution at that time to honor and pay permitted transactions were higher than the amount effectively granted to said banking institution by the Central Bank, for which it was necessary for it to use other sources of funds in order to cover that difference in permitted transactions."*

"In fact, from the very analysis, it is determined that, during the same period, Filanbanco obtained funds from sources other than the Central Bank, all of which has led the Lending Entity to act in the secure knowledge that the funds that were being authorized and that were authorized were appropriately utilized by the borrow-

ing financial institution to cover permissible transactions."

In spite of this, the Chief Prosecutor initially ordered an investigation of an alleged offense, which served to initiate the trial on the bases of supposed "bank embezzlement". Later on, in November of 2002, once the Attorney General's Office had completed an exhaustive investigation, compiled documents and taken statements, the Prosecutor, in correct application of the law, dismissed the charges of "bank embezzlement" and sustained the charge of "falsification of documents," which only had to do with the formal method of presenting the balances and did not have the criminal implications of embezzlement, which could be subject to bail while the corresponding trial moved forward.

The Chief Justice of the Supreme Court at that time, Armando Bermeo, did not take the Chief Prosecutor's decision into account and decided four months later, in March of 2003, to take the entrepreneurs, Roberto and William Isaias, to full trial. The Chief Justice considered that, if there had not been "bank embezzlement" when the Central Bank of Ecuador monitored the liquidity loans to Filanbanco, perhaps it had been committed earlier. Embezzlement in the management of private funds in a private bank was just a legal rebuff, but that did not matter. Relentless persecution at the highest level was now guaranteed more than ever. The Chief Justice of the Supreme Court and the Superintendent of Banks were from the same political party and both were members of the ministerial cabinet of President Rodrigo Borja between 1988 and 1992, the first as Legal Secretary and the second as Minister of Industry and Commerce.

From that moment on, absolutely any possibility of an objective, level-headed and legal trial went up in smoke. No judge or prosecutor could even insinuate that due process would be guaranteed because he or she would be persecuted. On the basis of the ruling proffered by the Chief Prosecutor, the Committee for Civic Control of Corruption (CCCC) requested that the Chief Justice of the Supreme Court, Dr. Galo Pico Mantilla, initiate a criminal trial against Dr. Yepez and her advisor, Dr. Washington Pesantez, for breach of public duty for allegedly delaying the criminal procedures against the Isaias brothers. Likewise, she was called to appear before Congress in a political trial for "having absolved the Isaias'." The trial was not successful when she explained that the investigated facts did not justify the charges of embezzlement, and furthermore, that such a violation did not exist in December of 1998.

Years later, in 2007, when Dr. Yepez was no longer the Chief Prosecutor, she still had to face certain columnists from newspapers like El Universo, which had published in its May 5th edition that, in November of 2002, she had reduced the charges of embezzlement to falsification of documents. In a letter sent to this newspaper, Dr. Yepez asked the author of the article how it was possible to reduce a crime, and noted: "...the banking crisis was also used for notoriety and publicity by avid false leaders... This trial, which became emblematic due to self-interests and passions, has gone on for five years without even finishing the first phase; nevertheless, no one has been challenged..."

PRESIDENTS ALSO PERSECUTE

From the moment of the economic crisis that forged Filanbanco to accept liquidity credit from the Central Bank in 1998 up until July of 2010, the Republic of Ecuador has had five constitutional Presidents: Jamil Mahuad, Gustavo Noboa, Lucio Gutierrez, Alfredo Palacio and Rafael Correa. Although the majority of them did not intervene, not even to guarantee "due process," the least that one could ask for in a lawful State, in large part due to the enormous politicization of the case that would surely have affected their presidential approval ratings, Lucio Gutierrez and Rafael Correa did intervene openly.

Gutierrez, in the middle of the political crisis, seeking to ingratiate himself with certain economic sectors and the media, which had always viewed the tragedy of the Isaias with complacency, dismissed the Supreme Court of Justice in April of 2005. The motivation for this dismissal lay in the fact that the Criminal Chambers of the Court was preparing a ruling absolving the Isaias. Gutierrez did not take heed of the harm that his measure did to the country's institutionalism. He abruptly shattered the equilibrium between the powers, but he felt that any decision he made during his term could be tolerated by the political and business class, except for absolving the ex-shareholders of Filanbanco. President Lucio Gutierrez had to face serious riots and demonstrations demanding his resignation. He lost the support of the Joint Command of the Armed Forces and took asylum in the Brazilian Embassy. Congress declared a presidential vacancy and appointed Alfredo Palacio as his replacement.

RAFAEL CORREA AND THE SEIZURE OF THE GROUP'S COMPANIES

President Rafael Correa Delgado, born in Guayaquil on April 6th of 1963, assumed the Ecuadorian presidency on January 15th of 2007, in the name of the political movement, Alianza PAIS (the Alliance for a High and Sovereign State). Correa, a left-wing economist, won the presidential elections without having much political experience and based his government program on reestablishing the State and Ecuadorian democracy, through fortification of the institutions, prioritization of social expenses, energetic and financial sovereignty and a constituent process that would entrust him with governance, as his movement had not elected any members to Congress.

As a child, Correa, who was born into a devoutly Catholic, lower middle class family, had to endure the drama of his father's incarceration in a North American jail for three years on charges of drug trafficking. During the referendum campaign that would guarantee the election of a Constituent Assembly, he explained it in the following way: "...I had a very difficult childhood. When I was five years old, my father, who was unemployed, carried drugs to the United States and was taken prisoner. He was a victim of the system, not a criminal; he was just an unemployed man desperately trying to put food on the table."

Correa completed all of his studies in Catholic institutions, earning very high grades, which enabled him to receive a postgraduate scholarship from the Belgian government and the United States Agency for International Development (USAID).

Without having enlisted in the army, his only political experience with high bureaucracy at the ministerial cabinet level was when the President of the Republic, Alfredo Palacio (2005-2007), appointed him as Minister of Economics and Finance. Correa spent less than four months in this position, but it was enough for him to become a presidential candidate. It was also enough to demonstrate his left-wing radicalism and his ambivalence on many topics. At the beginning of his term as a Minister, he stated that the dollar would continue to be the Ecuadorian currency, but that he considered dollarization to be the greatest error of his country's financial policy. Although in the long run, he accepted that this measure could be reversed, he claimed that it would be very difficult to do so and that the government was not "suicidal." In Congress, he submitted a bill to reform the Fund for Stabilization, Social and Productive Investment and Reduction of Public Debt (FEIREP), which had the purpose of collecting excess petroleum profits and using 70% of the funds to pay external and internal public debt. The FEIREP was transformed into the Fund for Productive and Social Reactivation of Scientific and Technological Development and Fiscal Stabilization, which was allocated in the following way: 35% for lines of credit, 30% for social programs, 5% for scientific research, 5% for highway administration, 5% for environmental protection and the remaining 20% for stabilization of the petroleum industry. He criticized the petroleum policies of his predecessors as "disastrous" and "marked by betrayal of the country."

Populism and demagogy were at the top of his political to-do list from the beginning of his campaign, identifying him with Chavez and Evo Morales. As he became more popular, he also became more outspoken. Wearing a poncho and a sombrero, he appeared in the village of Zumbahua at 11,500 feet above sea level and announced his intention to run for President. His critics emphasized his populist behavior, his fashionable rejection of the FTA with the Americans and even the similarity of his speeches to those of former Presidents Bucaram and Gutierrez, although they were not exactly his role models.

His political movement, Alianza PAIS, was officially unveiled in Quito on February 19th of 2006, and in his first speech as a candidate, he announced what would be a fundamental part of his activities: "dealing the death blow to traditional party politics." His left-wing tendencies were reaffirmed during his visits with various Latin American leaders. He attended the presidential inauguration of Evo Morales in January of 2006, and in February, he participated in the VIII International Conference of Economists in Havana. He visited Nestor Kirchner at his presidential headquarters and met with Chavez in Caracas after giving a conference at Venezuela's Bolivarian University.

Correa won the election, and on January 15th of 2007, he took over as President of the Republic, but not before first having been symbolically inaugurated on the 14th by the indigenous community of Zumbahua, which he had visited before and which had given him the baton, the poncho and the sombrero, representing the three traditional attributes of power. Evo Morales and Hugo Chavez were two of the out-of-the ordinary witnesses to this ceremony.

In the first speech of his term, Rafael Correa proclaimed the beginning of the "Citizens' Revolution" and called for a mass consultation on the election of a constituent assembly. The legal mechanisms used to dismiss 57 members of Congress accused of "interfering in the election process" of this convocation did not affect his popularity, and on September 30th of 2007 with a 73.2% voter turnout, the Ecuadorian people gave Correa his victory with 69.5% of the vote, and he elected 80 constituents out of 130 candidates. This triumph guaranteed the drafting of the new Magna Carta and the President's basic objective of reestablishing the Ecuadorian State.

Correa continued to reaffirm his well-earned label as a populist, not only by what he said, but also by his actions. He threatened the Ecuadorians with his resignation if he should lose the "yes" vote on the election of the Constituent Assembly. He did not renew the agreement with the United States on the Manta Air Base. During his campaign, he had said: "If I am President, I would cut off my hand before I would renew that agreement." However, this calculated hatred for the "Empire" was not enough for him to oppose the law for Andean Commercial Promotion and Eradication of Drugs (ATPDEA), through which the American government granted Ecuador, as a member of the Andean region, preferential tariffs on the country's imports in exchange for its commitment to the war on drugs.

Furthermore, his decision not to submit lists to Congress at the time of the presidential elections had to do not only with his plans to later dismiss its members through the Constituent Assembly, but also with his aversion to party politics, the neo-liberal model and the reign of a democracy that was exclusive and corrupt with its spoils system. This was also evident in his words on the day of his triumph: "The long neo-liberal night has ended," "The Playdoh democracy is over," and, "The dignified and socialist democracy of the 21st Century is beginning to rise."

THE SEIZURES

Correa's comportment toward the Isaias Group can be understood within the context of his populist behavior and the confrontation that had been created and deepened demagogically between the people and the "pelucones" especially in Guayaquil. It was the fight that invoked the people against the oligarchy. Against this backdrop, as soon as the President assumed office, he announced the creation of a committee to investigate the "bank robbery" of 1998-1999. He spared no disobliging phrases, such as "corrupt bankers" when referring to Filanbanco's ex-shareholders, discrediting them before the investigation was even completed.

The committee appointed by the President lacked the capacity to carry out an impartial investigation, as Correa had already gotten the judges' attention when there were rumors that the Isaias' were going to be absolved. Roberto Isaias recalls the presidential admonition: "...We must be very careful about the country's judges because, look out! They are making rulings in favor of those corrupt bankers." Correa's attitude and behavior, which demonstrate clear interference in justice, stand in marked contrast to the position assumed by the President when he was questioned in 2010 by the BBC in London as to whether or not the Colombian President Elect, Juan Manuel Santos, could visit Ecuador. He responded: "As long as there is a warrant and the case is still open, it is not possible." He added: "Justice is independent and there is nothing I can do. Of course, this trial and the prison sentence are going to be a problem. Hopefully Ecuadorian justice will resolve it as quickly as possible, but I could never interfere in the functioning of the Judicial System in Ecuador."

Roberto Isaias still recalls how Pedro Delgado, who in June of 2000 held the position of National Intendant of Supervision of Financial Entities, returned to the scene of the "Filanbanco Case" in 2008, convincing the President that the assets of the Isaias' could be seized.

That is exactly what happened. On July 8th of 2008, in accordance with Article 29 of the Law of Economic and Tax Reform, the Deposit Guarantee Agency (AGD) ordered the seizure of all the assets of the administrators and ex-shareholders of Filanbanco as of December 2nd of 1998, for losses determined by the Banking Board to be 661 million dollars, in accordance with the provisions of Ruling JB-2008-01084 of February 26th of 2008.

More than 150 companies were seized, including agricultural, commercial, insurance and construction companies, as well as media. They seized yachts that were not used for commercial purposes and a personal collection of antique cars. Many of the companies were not even part of the Isaias Group. TC Television belonged to Estefano Isaias, who had nothing to do with the

Filanbanco Case, given that there were no charges against him and he had acquired the channel 10 years earlier. Additionally, Alvaro Dassum said that he, and not the Isaias brothers, was the owner of Gamavision. The Minister of Economics at that time, Fausto Ortiz de la Cadena, resigned from his post for disagreeing with this action and considering the measures taken by the AGD to be illegal.

The measure never ceased to elicit comments from both friends and opponents of the government. Juan Falconi Puig, a characterized personal enemy of the Group and the one responsible for the measures that led Filanbanco to insolvency while it was under government control, made no effort to hide his satisfaction with the measure, which freed him from blame and responsibility, stating: "...Too much time had passed, with unfortunate consequences for thousands of people who trusted Filanbanco, and most of all for the State. Now, with this measure, we have initiated a process of justice and punishment for those who bilked all of Ecuador out of a billion dollars." (www.hoy.com.ec) There was nothing strange about this pronouncement, as it was the same one he made 10 years earlier. He blamed the Group in order to save himself.

The editor of a newspaper, one of those that echoed the statements of the former President of the AGD, whose name was not published, reacted to the measure in this way: "I wanted to put this notice in the front-page headlines. I have waited for it anxiously, but no government since 1998 has done it."

In certain sectors opposed to the government, the greatest distrust of the measure arose from the seizure of the media, TC Television, Gamavision and Cablevision. There was suspicion that the government, in a full campaign for the "yes" vote on the referendum, would utilize the channels for official propaganda. In effect, that is what happened. Correa appointed his closest collaborators to these media: Enrique Arosemena Robles, who was the Director of Ecuador's government station, was made Director of the TV channels, and Jose Toledo, who was his press assistant during the campaign, was made Vice-President of News.

Vicente Taiano from the PRIAN political movement expressed that the measure against the Isaias family had a political-electoral undercurrent. In his opinion, it was suspicious that the Executive Branch was the one to administer TC Television and Gamavision at the very time of the campaign for the electoral referendum.

The Mayor of Guayaquil, Jaime Nebot, likewise questioned the seizures that the AGD had approved. Jorge Vivanco Mendieta, a journalist for Diario Expreso published in Guayaquil, in addition to noting that the process for carrying out a seizure had violated legal procedures , expressed: "In politics, nothing is coincidental, as all of this just happens to coincide with the campaign for the 'yes' vote on the referendum, while the polls are saying 'no.' It's a curious detail that, among the seized assets, there are media. The government now has 10 media channels, a related Supreme Electoral Court and other media that are either closed or threatened." Vivanco added: "Don't be fooled by the tangled web of legal arguments through which the populist President of Ecuador, Rafael Correa, is trying to justify the seizure of more than 150 companies of an Ecuadorian financial group... The government seizure of all of these companies this week has a single purpose: to take over the Group's three TV stations and put them before staunch supporters of the government, assuring control of the principle media in order to win the referendum in September, which will allow Correa to be reelected for another term."

Correa's reaction was livid, and as always, accompanied by improprieties directed against the bankers and even against the workers. During a meeting in San Francisco Plaza in Quito, the President characterized those who stated that the seizure of the Isaias' television channels was an assault on freedom of expression in Ecuador as "underhanded defenders of the corrupt bankers." In response to criticism that the measure was a strategy to prevent the failure of the "yes" vote on the referendum, he claimed: "Once again we're going to raid the coffers of the salaried employees of corrupt banking and those who oppose the changes we are making."

Through the seizures, the goal of the AGD and the Banking Board of Ecuador was to recover the money that was supposed they owed to Filanbanco's accountholders. They said that with the first group of seized companies they would only cover 260 million dollars, and the second of these estimated the Isaias Group's debt at 661 million dollars.

The recovery of funds through the sale of the seized assets has not happened to date because the government has simply kept the companies. The first instance of this is the case of Filanbanco, itself, which the government decided to keep when it was in optimal condition to be sold, and with that, unleashed all of the legal mess that has accompanied the case, and which the government, itself, has solved through political persecution of the bank's former shareholders.

Some journalists, commentators from various newspapers, have referred to the seizure process as follows: "Regardless of whether the Isaias Group – led by the brothers Roberto and William

Isaias – was responsible for embezzlement and fled to the U.S. to escape a trial, or whether – as the Isaias brothers state – they were victims of an economic crisis that led to the insolvency of nearly 30 Ecuadorian banks that year, the way in which the television stations in Ecuador were seized demonstrates all the characteristics of a brutal government attack against the freedom of the press." The writer adds: "If the seizure of the Isaias Group's television channels, which capture 40% of the evening news audience, were simply a financial decision for purposes of liquidating the assets and paying the creditors, Correa would have asked an accounting firm to appoint an independent director for them. Let's not forget that the President put two of his closest friends in charge of these channels, more for purposes of creating a favorable opinion of the government than for preparing the way for the channels' sale."

Another illustration of the fact that the government kept the companies is related by the journalist Manuel Ignacio Gomez with regard to the newspaper El Telegrafo: "When the AGD took possession of the newspaper, El Telegrafo, they told us that they would sell it to a private owner in order to compensate damages arising from the defunct Banco del Progreso. However, El Telegrafo was never sold, or rather it was 'sold' to the State, which is the same thing as not selling it. It became a public newspaper of the government. Not only did the State fail to recover accountholders' money by not selling the newspaper, but maintaining and modernizing it actually costs the State money, that is, it cost us, the Ecuadorian people, and all so that a few readers could quickly skim its pages. Did El Telegrafo even reach a thousand subscriptions? How much was spent per reader to maintain the newspaper? As of yesterday when I looked at it, there was nothing but State advertisements, which is the same as no advertisements. What a wonderful sale of El Telegrafo! What a wonderful recuperation of funds!"

The government has not sold a single one of the seized companies. It has appointed personal friends to manage them, regardless of whether or not they have administrative capabilities or knowledge of the related business or commercial sector. The appointments to these companies are nothing more than the President's way of paying political favors with high salaries, in detriment to the efficient administrative and financial operations the companies had at the time of their seizure. Meanwhile, the companies are being devaluated, are deteriorating, are losing their competitive edge and are on their way to being closed. Even the demagogical experiment with the Ramada Hotel has failed. The hotel workers were promised the shares and now they are in trust. Reports abound of the corrupt way in which the seized businesses have been managed.

THE DECISION OF THE AGD AND MANDATE No. 13

On the basis of regulations issued in the year 2002, in an attempt to regulate actions that happened back in 1998, the AGD issued the decision known as AGD-UIO-GG-2008-12 on July 8th of 2008, in accordance with Article 29 of the Law of Economic and Tax Reform. This law states: "...In those cases where the administrators have declared unrealistic technical property, have altered the figures in their balance sheets or have charged interest on interest, they will use their personal resources to guarantee the deposits of the financial institution, and the Deposit Guarantee Agency may seize those assets that are publicly known to be the property of those shareholders and hold them in trust while their true ownership is being determined.

With this decision, they proceeded to seize the Isaias Group's companies, but once the decision was known by the Group's lawyers, they contested the lien on the assets, which led to the enactment of Mandate No. 13. Constituent Mandate No. 13 was issued in a plenary session of the Constituent Assembly on July 9th of 2008.

The Constituent Assembly's haste to issue the Mandate, only 24 hours after the AGD's decision, had two fundamental objectives. The first was to correct certain irregularities in the latter, given that it was issued without the signature of the President of the Board of Directors and Minister of Finances, Fausto Ortiz de la Cadena, making it invalid.

Minister Ortiz had not signed the decision because he did not agree with it and considered it to be illegal. Under those circumstances, he tendered his resignation. The second objective was to block, in an absolutely unconstitutional way, any legal possibility of the decision being contested or made subject to any type of protection under the Constitution.

THE AGD FILES A SUIT IN MIAMI

The seizures of the Isaias' assets by the AGD in Ecuador after July 8th of 2008 did not seem to satisfy either the government nor the AGD's Manager, Carlos Bravo, as the latter, acting as Collections Court Judge, requested the Eleventh Circuit Court of Miami-Dade to freeze 20 million dollars' worth of the Ecuadorian businessmen's assets, which had been identified in Dade County, Florida.

The Isaias brothers countersued through their lawyers. A short time later, in July of 2010, Judge Gill S. Freeman of the Dade Circuit Court denied the AGD's motion to remove certain elements of the countersuit that they considered to be "immaterial, impertinent and scandalous." Likewise, she denied the AGD's petition to limit the action to the 22 companies of the ex-bankers that had been identified in the County, and on the contrary, allowed other companies affected by the State seizures to be included. Roberto Isaias points out that, in an international setting, this makes an excellent case for the supposition that the seizures carried out by the AGD were part of the political persecution strategy against the Group. (El Universo 8/7/2010)

The AGD remained active until December 31st of 2009. In a July 2010 interview with Ecuador Inmediato.Com, its former Manager, Carlos Bravo, with the characteristic cynicism of those who acted against the Group, expressed that it seemed strange to him that the assets still had not been sold two years after the seizure.

In the interview, the ex-manager said: "...It isn't that those seizures were made simply to make them; not at all. Those seizures had a sole purpose. This was the purpose established in the Law of Economic and Tax Reform, which fundamental objective was: to compensate those who suffered damages due to those bankers and, furthermore, to compensate the Ecuadorian State for the money used to save the banks."

He also added that, in his opinion, there was no valid pretext for not having sold the assets to date, but he failed to explain why he did not sell them when he was in charge of the AGD: "Furthermore, we, I, as Manager of the AGD, while I was reconstituting the Deposit Guarantee Agency, which I had found in tatters, literally, completely devastated, with missing files, no institutional records, nothing, because they were stealing reports, well anyway, everything that they were doing in this sad Deposit Guarantee Agency, which was a bad idea in the first place... But, well, that's another story... While I was doing that, I carried out the seizures, and after three months, I had already had the principle seized businesses appraised." He also asserts: "...The money could not be returned to the accountholders. Why? Because the seized companies had not been sold."

Once the AGD was eliminated, the Minister of Economics and Finances assumed the duties related to seizures and carried out the last one in June, seizing personal property of the Isaias brothers. This time, an antique car collection and yachts for personal use were seized. The media circus was impressive. Television, radio and the press all followed the seizures and the cars were paraded through the streets of various cities in a full-fledged spectacle. The seized property was displayed as if it were goods stolen by a band of thieves that had been recovered by the police, as if they had not been purchased with the buyers' own funds that were the fruit of honorable labor.

5

THE POLITICIZATION OF JUSTICE: THE VIOLATION OF DUE PROCESS AGAINST THE ISAIAS'

When asked by Ramon Jimeno (Jimeno 2006:195) whether he felt like the victim of persecution by a man or by a system, Roberto Isaias responded as follows: "I feel like a victim of persecution by the media, by people, by certain political parties and by Presidents at that time who wanted to base their political campaigns on the crisis in the financial system because they believed that was the best way to win the election. My brother and I have been used as part of political campaigns, political games and persecution on the part of certain political parties."

Transformed by the media into the "Filanbanco Case," the case against the Isaias Group elicited the basest sentiments of their detractors. Envy, hatred and vengeance have flourished throughout a decade against a family group that, from generation to generation, promoted the economic development of broad geographic sectors in Ecuador, created employment, imported modern technology, improving the performance of local industry, and showed the way to business success, nurtured by virtues, such as laboriousness, dedication, sacrifice, loyalty and persistence.

The political class considered that demagogic, populist and classist expressions tinged with hatred for "the pelucones" could bear fruit and votes, and took advantage of this. All of the State's legal resources were mobilized against the Group, to accuse, to indict, to impede impartial justice, to draw out processes, to disallow absolution, to enter orders for preventive custody, to seize and even to prevent the Group or its lawyers from seeking protection in the Constitution.

The media of the Group's competitors, the ones in the State's hands and those that were tied to the interests of political groups were all committed to spreading false information about Filanbanco. In an effort to influence the opinion of television viewers, radio listeners and newspaper readers, they spread the notion that those responsible for the country's financial collapse were the Isaias'. The magnitude of the crisis did not matter. The fact that Filanbanco closed its doors while it was under administration by the State did not matter. What did matter was taking advantage of a propitious opportunity to eliminate the competition, even if it meant back-stabbing.

If there is any special characteristic that stands out in the "Filanbanco Case," differentiating it from all of the financial and legal maneuvers carried out during banking crises in the world's democratic countries with free enterprise and private property, it is that, up to now, the Isaias Group has not had any opportunity for due process. On the contrary, laws have been enacted expressly in order to affect the Isaias' personal situation.

Due process is today considered to be one of the most important conquests in humankind's fight for the respect of fundamental rights. It is a tenet of the legal process, which grants every person the right to certain minimal guarantees, aimed at ensuring a fair result within that process and providing the opportunity to be heard before a judge. Its origins go back to the Magna Carta of King John of England in 1215, which in Clause 48 established that "no free man shall be seized or imprisoned, or stripped of his rights or possessions, or outlawed or exiled, or deprived of his standing in any other way, nor will we proceed with force against him, or send others to do so, except by the lawful judgment of his equals or by the law of the land." The United States Constitution incorporated the concept of due process in 1791, through the 5th and 14th Amendments, which establish that "no person shall...be deprived of life, liberty or property without due process of law."

The Universal Declaration of Human Rights, approved by the Assembly of the United Nations on December 10th of 1948, includes the essential elements of due process in two clauses. In Article 8, it establishes: "...Everyone has the right to an effective remedy by the competent national tribunals for acts violating the fundamental rights granted him by the constitution or by law." In Article 10, it states: "...Everyone is entitled in full equality to a fair and public hearing by an independent and impartial tribunal, in the determination of his rights and obligations and of any criminal charge against him."

Due process as a personal guarantee was incorporated into most of the world's political constitutions during the 20th Century. The Ecuadorian Constitution (1998) in Article 24 states the following: "In order to ensure due process, the following basic guarantees must be observed, without prejudice to others established by the Constitution, international treaties, the law or jurisprudence." This article is composed of 17 items, among which we will point out the first, which is relevant to the case of the Isaias family and which states: "No one may be judged for an act or omission that, at the moment of its commission, is not legally typified as a criminal, administrative or other type of violation, nor may a punishment be applied that is not envisaged in the Constitution or the Law. Likewise, a person may not be judged except in accordance with preexisting laws, with observance of the process corresponding to each proceeding." Item 17 states: "Every person shall have the right to access the legal system and to obtain effective, impartial and expedited counsel in his or her rights and interests from the same, without remaining defenseless under any circumstances. Failure to comply with the legal decisions will be punished under the law."

Additionally, the Ecuadorian Constitution, in certain cases, such as that considered in Article 77, Item 1, empowers the judge to order precautionary measures other than preventive custody, or as established in Item 11, authorizes the judge to apply alternative punishments and precautionary measures to incarceration in a prioritized manner, as established by Law. With regard to the "Rights to Protection," the Constitution states that a motion for extraordinary protection submitted before the Constitutional Court is appropriate in the case of definitive sentences or rulings in which rights acknowledged in the Constitution have been violated through an action or omission.

Lastly, the Constitution states in Article 11, Item 9: "...The State shall be liable for arbitrary detention, legal error, unjustified delays, inadequate administration of justice, violation of the right to effective legal counsel, and violations of the principles and rules of due process."

Anyone would think that, since Ecuador is a democracy, a lawful State that respects the "due process" established in its political Constitution, no one should be afraid to submit him or herself to justice. However, in the trial of the Isaias brothers, there is irrefutable evidence of a perverse politicization of justice, which has completely violated all the rules of due process from the very beginning. Without yet embarking on the purely legal analysis, it is worth noting these facts in light of the provisions of the Constitution.

Roberto and William Isaias are on trial for "bank embezzlement." This crime was not typified in the Ecuadorian Penal Code at the time that it supposedly occurred. Here we have the first example of deviation from the Political Manifest, which states: "No one may be judged for an act or omission that, at the moment of its commission, is not legally typified as a criminal violation..." It was an invention and a contribution to the Penal Code by Superintendent Falconi in order to initiate his persecution and collection account against the Isaias'. Embezzlement is only committed by public officials who avail of State resources. Filanbanco was a private financial institution until December 2nd of 1998. As such, up to that moment, the bank's shareholders could not have committed embezzlement, and the liquidity loans were monitored by the Central Bank, as we have already seen, in spite of Filanbanco still being privately owned. After December 2nd, Filanbanco became an official institution under State administration. If "embezzlement" occurred during this new phase, the culprits must be sought within the AGD, which was administering the bank.

The political persecution violated fundamental principles of democracy, such as the division of powers. The Judicial Branch was subjugated to the Executive Branch and the Legislative Branch, which was commissioned to legislate against the entrepreneurs by naming a new crime when necessary. Laws were being reformed and adapted at the rate that was required by the political vendetta, and in such a way that the Isaias brothers had no access to any legal remedy in their favor. It cannot be denied that the economic crisis found the Superintendence of Banks, the Central Bank and other financial authorities without legal recourse, and as such, it was necessary to reform the laws and adapt them to the new reality. What has no legal basis is that the laws were reformed and then applied retroactively against the Isaias'. From a perspective of law and due process, all of this is simply aberrant. Let's look at the principle laws and legal remedies that have been used specifically to persecute the Isaias Group:

Law 99-26 Reform of the General Law of Institutions in the Financial System, of the Law of Economic and Tax Reform and of the Penal Code

This law was published in Official Registry No. 190 of May 13th of 1999. It constitutes the first link of the chain making up the demonization, persecution and politicization of justice against the Isaias brothers. It was presented to society as the legal solution to the wrongdoings of "corrupt banking," and typified actions that were previously permissible as new crimes, such as granting credit to affiliates up to the legal limit. Introducing *"bank embezzlement"* into the legal definition of embezzlement, punishing administrators, executives and employees of private banks for the misuse of funds is a clear judgment of reproach and an implicit social condemnation of previous banking activity. This legal reform would be the key tool for persecuting the Isaias brothers by applying it retroactively in clear violation of the principle of legality and the grandfather clause of criminal law. Its most notable reforms were:

a. It supplanted Article 73 of the General Law of the Financial System, prohibiting all transactions with individuals or legal entities *affiliated* with the administration or owners of a financial institution, its subsidiaries or Parent Corporation. These transactions were previously authorized up to a legal limit. It was applied retroactively against the Isaias', who had performed transactions of this type within permissible limits.

b. It added a third section to Article 257 of the Penal Code, introducing what was denominated as *bank embezzlement* into the legal description of *embezzlement* and extending criminal liability to the officers, administrators, executives and employees of the national private financial system, as well as to any members or spokespersons of the Board of Directors of these entities who may have participated in the commission of these illicit acts.

Charges of bank embezzlement were retroactively applied against Roberto and William Isaias without any grounds. The amendment to the Code is from 1999 and they turned Filanbanco over to the AGD on December 2nd of 1998.

c. It added Article 257, Item A to the Penal Code, which typifies the crime of malicious concession or acquisition of credit to or by affiliated companies, violating express legal provisions with regard to this type of transaction.

The criminal trial against the Filanbanco shareholders, initiated in 2000

Without knowledge of the legal and technical realities surrounding the Filanbanco Case, as exemplified by the Restructuring Agreement for the fortification and patrimonial solvency of the bank, the economist Pedro Delgado, the National Intendant of Supervision of Financial Entities, issued a report at the request of Juan Falconi Puig, a declared enemy of the Isaias family and the one who, at that time, held the position of Superintendent of Banks. This report with allegations of illicit acts was sent to the District Attorney, marking the beginning of the criminal investigation of the Isaias' for embezzlement (case No. 57-2000).

This criminal case is full of irregularities and violations of human rights. At this point, we will point out the following examples:

a. *Omission of required grounds for prosecution*: The investigation began without the General Comptroller of the State performing a prior special examination and informing the court of any *"indications of criminal liability"* on the part of the persons to be tried. Having grounds for prosecution is an indispensable requirement for initiating a criminal investigation.

b. *The legal definition of embezzlement*: The term "embezzlement" refers to a felony typified in Article 257 of the Penal Code. Conceived exclusively as a crime pertaining to public officials, it was extended in 1999 to include the administrators of private banks, coining the term "bank embezzlement."

In effect, Article 257 punishes the general "misuse of public funds." The penal doctrine is clear in determining that these misuses are distinct from: (i) **larceny** (the removal of funds); (ii) **mi-**

sappropriation (different or undue application of funds); (iii) **temporary embezzlement** (the temporary removal of funds with the intention of reimbursing them); and (iv) **retention** (non-payment of funds).

Misappropriation, or using funds for a public purpose other than that which was originally intended, has been decriminalized in many countries of the world for its lack of legal severity. Ecuador decriminalized it through Supreme Decree No. 1429 in Official Registry No. 337 of May 16th of 1997, which deleted the word "misappropriation" from the legal description of embezzlement. Once misappropriation, also known as "different or unwarranted public investment," was decriminalized, it could no longer be included under the generic definition "misuse of public funds," which has always existed in the criminal definition of embezzlement.

c. *Formal audit and preliminary investigation*: The formal audit and the preliminary investigation in this case considered all of the possible ways to commit embezzlement: (i) Investigators sought indications of larceny in the legitimate authorization of loans to affiliated companies. These loans were legally permitted and regulated until 1999, the year in which they were prohibited and typified as a crime. (ii) Investigators sought indications of misappropriation in any unauthorized use of the liquidity loans from the Central Bank of Ecuador (BCE) that were granted for purposes of turning the bank around. All suspicions were invalidated, primarily through the technical and documental evidence issued by the control authorities, themselves, the Superintendence of Banks and the BCE. There are notable examples of collaboration and favorable legal opinion in defense of the syndicates of the Isaias family on the part of important national professors and lawyers, particularly Dr. Juan Larrea Holguin, the Archbishop of Guayaquil and one of the most distinguished and important essayists that Ecuador has produced.

d. *The charges of the District Attorney*: After analyzing the evidence from the preliminary investigation, the District Attorney, who is the only person authorized to formulate charges by the Attorney General, Dr. Mariana Yepez, accused Roberto and William Isaias and other defendants of the minor crime of falsification or alteration of balance sheets, owing to certain inaccuracies that these records allegedly reflected during the time of the crisis, through a criminal filing dated June 16th of 2000.

Civil trial No. 147-D-2001 in the Third Civil Court of Guayaquil

On March 14th of 2001, through the companies that were former shareholders in Filanbanco, S.A., the Isaias family filed a civil suit in the amount of 158,000,000 U.S. dollars against the Deposit Guarantee Agency (AGD), demanding the assets (the portfolio or client debts) that were amortized against the countable capital balance and other patrimonial accounts of the private ex-shareholders, which were never delivered by the Deposit Guarantee Agency in spite of being expressly and imperatively established in Article 24, Item D of the Law of Economic and Tax Reform, which was in effect at that time. This fair legal claim was immediately demonized by adversaries of the Isaias family and the government, giving it the pejorative nickname, "*the turnabout trial.*"

Finally, through a legal ruling of August 27th of 2001, entered into the record and made executable, the judge of competence acknowledged that the legal subrogation was in favor of the ex-shareholders of Filanbanco, S.A., expressing this in the seventh recital of the ruling.

The unfavorable reaction of Ecuadorian governmental organizations to the measure was immediate:

1. Through a ruling of September 7th of 2001, the Banking Board of Ecuador vainly tried to modify the legal decision, excluding the assets that are recorded in the sentence of Ruling No. 147.

2. The judge who issued the ruling was dismissed from office by the National Judiciary Council.

3. Law No. 2002-60 was enacted on January 28th of 2002 in order to interfere in the legal decision in this case, ignoring the final and binding nature of the ruling and the principle of *res judicata*. However, the judge that replaced the exonerated judicial officer, exercising the powers of general constitutional control, declared the inapplicability of the provisions of Law 2002-60 to Ruling No. 147-D-2001.

4. Through Ruling AGD-UIO-GG-2008-035 of August 12th of 2008, the Deposit Guarantee Agency seized the rights of Filanbanco's ex-shareholders stemming from Ruling No. 147-D-2001.

The President's refusal to object to the provisions of the bill that gave rise to Law No. 2002-60

This bill had the goal of persecuting the Isaias brothers and trying to cancel the effects of the executable decision pronounced in Ruling No. 147-D-2001, which declared that the legal subrogation of Filanbanco's creditor rights was in favor of the former private shareholders, with regard to the credits (client debts) that were amortized with the patrimonial accounts of the ex-shareholders in the amount of 158,000,000 U.S. dollars.

The President of the Republic, Dr. Gustavo Novoa Bejarano, in a veto document or *partial objection* to this bill, acknowledged expressly and in detail that this bill was targeted, that it contained unconstitutional regulations and that its provisions threatened *legal security*. He established this without reservations in the document; however, for political reasons, he neglected to formally veto or object to those provisions, which he had subjected to extensive legal analysis in the text.

For this reason, the bill for Law No. 2002-60 was processed in full knowledge of its many unconstitutionalities and the fact that it was targeted toward certain people, as detailed in the previously mentioned document, **signed on December 28th of 2001** by the President of the Republic at that time, Dr. Gustavo Noboa Bejarano. This document states:

"It is evident that objecting to the unconstitutionality of various provisions dictated by the members of different political currents, in many cases, the same ones who brought about the country's banking debacle upon approving the law that is being reformed today, would have a significant political impact. In effect, in full knowledge that the law is clearly targeted and that its approval by the National Congress would be threatening to legal security, the legislators have attempted to leave the historical responsibility for objecting to such provisions in the hands of the Executive Branch

in an attempt to make me politically responsible for the effects of this objection. What is even worse politically is that they have invited me to approve these provisions, which would unquestionably destroy the legal security that is essential for the various social and productive sectors, with immeasurable ramifications that would threaten the Nation's future and its progress."

For political reasons, President Noboa Bejarano's hands were trembling and he neglected to exercise his constitutional powers to veto or object to such provisions in the process of creating laws. He did this with full knowledge and in the exercise of his official duties, through a politically calculated omission, and by doing so, allowed the persecution of the Isaias family.

Law No. 2002-60 Reforms to the Law of Economic and Tax Reform, the Law of Monetary and Banking Procedures and the State Bank and the General Law of Institutions in the Financial System

These reforms were published in the supplement to Official Registry No. 503 of the 28th of January of 2002.

This law was another link in the chain of persecution. It came about after the executable legal sentence dated August 27th of 2001 in Ruling No. 147-2001, which stated that the legal subrogation of the creditor rights to client debt, which was amortized against the patrimonial accounts of Fi-

114

lanbanco's ex-shareholders on December 2nd of 1998, was in favor of the former shareholders. This law ignores the validity and effect of the judicial ruling and the principle of *res judicata*, civilly, criminally and administratively publishing any public official, including judges, who in any way contradict it or attempt to make Article 15 retroactive simply through a list of errata.

It is evident that Law No. 2002-60 was devious *ab initio*, but it is surprising that State officials did not approve its provisions and attempt to expand its arbitrariness, beyond its legal arbitrariness, as in the case of Carlos Bravo, the General Manager of the AGD, who wanted to make the personal patrimonial guarantee of the administrators of a financial institution retroactive, as established in Article 4 and not in Article 15, to which the above list of errata refers, with the sole intention of jeopardizing the Isaias brothers through this law, which was enacted on January 28th of 2002, while the Isaias' had forfeited Filanbanco on December 2nd of 1998. This law introduced the following:

a. Article 4 of this law replaced Article 29 of the Law of Economic and Tax Reform, and in its final section created the *personal patrimonial guarantee* of the administrators-shareholders of financial institutions that had made unrealistic statements of technical property, had altered figures in their balance sheets or had charged interest on interest. Likewise, it authorized the AGD's power to seize assets that are publicly known to be the property of these administrators-shareholders and hold them in trust while their true ownership is determined, in which case they would become AGD resources.

b. Article 15 of the same law adds a final section to Article 167 of the General Law of Institutions in the Financial System, which establishes: (i) that the shareholders, administrators, persons or companies linked to the financial institution, either through shares or another type of financial claim, may only collect on these claims out of any surplus remaining after the liquidation process is complete, and only after having satisfied all of the original, ceded or subrogated obligations; (ii) that no contract, trust, precautionary measure, administrative decision or *legal ruling* will be valid when it in any way contradicts this provision; (iii) that any person, company or legal representative of these, including debtors, guarantors, judges, control and administrative authorities and generally anyone who registers property and merchandise, who contravenes the dispositions of this legal regulation will be held criminally and civilly liable.

c. The list of errata, published in Official Registry No. 549 of April 5th of 2002, establishes that, on the fourth line of Article 20 of Law No. 2002-60, there is an error, where instead of saying

Article 14, it should say Article 15. In this unusual manner, it was attempted to *retroactively* apply the provisions of Article 15, which had become effective on the date on which the Law of Economic and Tax Reform was published in the Official Registry, that is, as of December 1st of 1998. On April 25th of 2002, the judge who pronounced Ruling No. 147-2001, exercising the powers of general control authorized by Article 274 of the 1998 Constitution, declared that Articles 15 and 20 of Law No. 2002-60 were unconstitutional.

Constituent Mandate No. 13, enacted in a plenary session of the Constituent Assembly on July 9th of 2008

Mandate No. 13 was published in the supplement to Official Registry No. 378 of August 11th of 2008. Of all the legal recourses utilized in the political and judicial persecution of Roberto and William, this one stands out the most. It was conceived and drafted at the request of a group of constituent assemblymen who were supporters of the government, who expressly requested and succeeded the same day to deny the Isaias brothers' access to justice, going against all of the principles and regulations of legal procedure and those of the human rights agreements signed and ratified by the Ecuadorian State.

Constituent Mandate No. 13 originated from a motion on July 9th of 2008 — one day after the

117

seizures — by a group of assemblymen close to the government, expressly targeted against the Isaias', and was approved the same day, with the clear goal of: (i) Attempting to rectify the improprieties and flaws that affected Ruling AGD-UIO-GG-2008; (ii) Impeding the Isaias family's access to legal counsel, for which purposes the motion was expressly intended; (iii) Criminally and civilly punishing any judge who admitted motions or other special actions appealing the constitutionality of the seizures; and (iv) Establishing that the AGD must apply Article 29 of the Law of Economic and Tax Reform to all of the shareholders and administrators of the banks that closed and were taken over by the AGD, and that are included in Article 29 of the same law.

This Mandate rectifies the flaws in the AGD ruling that served to authorize the seizure of the Isaias' companies and to leave the Isaias' without any possibility of turning to any instance or court in search of constitutional protection. It is the most significant violation of due process, and by extension, of the Ecuadorian Constitution and the Universal Declaration of Human Rights. It has no precedent in the legal history of Ecuador.

Constituent Mandates, like the one mentioned above, are legal regulations that the Constituent Assembly's Procedural Code empowered it to issue during its sessions, although the 1998 Constitution was still in effect. The provisions of Mandate No. 13 are:

Article 1: To ratify the full legal validity of Ruling AGD-UIO-2008-12 of July 8th of 2008, ordering the seizure of the assets of the former shareholders and administrators of Filanbanco, S.A. for purposes of returning the funds to the State and all the Ecuadorian people who continue to suffer damages from the insolvency of said bank.

Article 2: To declare that Ruling AGD-UIO-GG-2008-12 of July 8th of 2008, issued by the General Manager of the Deposit Guarantee Agency, is not subject to any motion for constitutional protection or of other special character, and if such a motion is made, it will be immediately dismissed without suspending or impeding the fulfillment of the abovementioned Ruling. Any judge or magistrate who hears and rules on any type of motion for unconstitutionality related to this ruling or who takes it upon himself to execute, implement or bring such motion to completion must make it inadmissible, under penalty of removal from office, without prejudice to any criminal liability that may apply.

Mandate No. 13 eliminated any possibility of legal recourse in the presence of a seizure process that was full of illegalities, and in which assets were also seized from persons who had

119

nothing to do with the Isaias' companies. For this reason, both in light of the 1998 Constitution and according to the provisions of the 2008 Constitution, it is evident that Constituent Mandate No. 13 is unconstitutional and violates the international treaties signed and ratified by Ecuador, which guarantee access to justice. Nevertheless, Mandate No. 13 was applied to impede any actions attempted in Ecuador by the Isaias family or its agents, in spite of the existence of express constitutional regulations that allow contesting administrative acts, that confer the right to legal counsel and that recognize the supremacy of constitutional regulations and rights, namely: Article 11, Item 4; Article 76, Item 7, Subsection A; Article 173; Article 424; Article 425 and Article 426 of the 2008 Constitution.

Extradition Law No. 2000-24

This law was published in Official Registry No. 152 of August 30th of 2000. It is yet another example of how laws were reformed in order to be applied in the persecution of the Isaias brothers.

This law was not innocuous; it was not enacted in order to bring the Isaias brothers to Ecuador and try them before an independent and impartial court of justice with the guarantee of applying the rules of due process, the law and the Constitution. The Isaias brothers were judged and condemned without a trial, by public opinion that had been manipulated by the government and the media in a determinate effort to make them appear responsible for the economic crisis and the closure of Filanbanco under government control.

After charges were filed against the Isaias', this law established that, in order to initiate an *active extradition* process, an order for *preventive custody* or an executable legal sentence would be required. As the existing regulations on active extradition in 2000, contained in the Regulations of the Immigration Law of June 30th of 1986, were only applicable in cases where there was already an executable legal sentence, and in the Isaias' case, there was only an order for preventive custody, it was necessary to reform the law in order to adapt it to the necessities of extraditing the businessmen.

The Chief Justice of the Supreme Court petitioned the United States for the active extradition of Roberto and William Isaias, based on the order for preventive custody. The administrative procedures for remitting documents through the diplomatic route were full of irregularities, including the remittance of documents that did not form part of the criminal process, exclusion of evidence of discharge, etc. The Ecuadorian authorities that have intervened in these official actions have demonstrated that they are willing to go to any lengths in order to succeed in extraditing the

Isaias brothers. This extradition procedure is currently in progress.

Executive Decree No. 914, which Reforms the Regulations of the Law on Travel Documents

The persecution against the Isaias brothers did not let up during the term of Rafael Correa. On the contrary, his speeches against the "corrupt bankers" became increasingly vehement. His close collaborators in the government had the opportunity to persecute the Isaias' with more even more brutality. First were the seizures in Ecuador, then the lawsuits and the retention of their passports in Miami.

Executive Decree No. 9114 was issued after William Isaias presented his passport in the Ecuadorian Consulate in Miami on January 29th of 2008, when both his old and new passports were illegally retained. The Decree established:

a. That the Ministry of Foreign Relations, its departments or consulate offices would abstain from granting passports to Ecuadorians who are fugitives from justice;

b. That for these purposes, the Ministry of the Government and Police would periodically provide a list with their names, copies of legal orders and other pertinent data in order to facilitate the identification of citizens who are fugitives from justice; and

c. That this decree would become effective upon its publication in the Official Registry.

This Decree went into effect on February 18th of 2008, in violation of the provisions of a legal regulation of superior hierarchy, namely, Article 4 of the Law of Travel Documents, which establishes that every Ecuadorian has the right to obtain a passport and that no authority may refuse to grant it whenever the legal requirements are fulfilled. To legally reform or modify this law, it would require another law that expressly orders such reforms, which cannot be made through a simple Executive Decree.

Ruling of the Directors of the AGD, Act No. 150 of July 4th of 2008

Without a sentence from a judge and without having concluded the criminal trial against the Isaias brothers, once again an administrative act was used to add another link to the chain of persecution. Although Act No. 150 gave the false impression of an act of justice against the rich in order to compensate society, in reality, its sole purpose was to confiscate the assets of the Isaias family, and most of all, to take over the conglomerate of media with the highest audience in the country and integrate these into the propaganda mechanism of President Rafael Correa, who at that time was carrying out a campaign for the referendum.

With regard to Act No. 150 of the Directors of the Deposit Guarantee Agency (AGD): (i) It is mendacious; it was falsely dated July 4th of 2008, stating that it was enacted in the Ministry of Economics at twelve forty, so that it could serve as a precedent for the orders for seizure that would be dictated by Carlos Bravo, the General Manager of the AGD on July 8th of 2008 and subsequently. The government press, more due to error than to objectivity, tells the true story on page 6 of the July 9th, 2008 edition of El Telegrafo, where it indicated a chronology of events and expressed that the order of the Directors of the AGD was dictated on July 7th at 9:00PM. (ii) There is no signature of the Minister of Finances, the economist Fausto Ortiz de la Cadena; the space is left blank, given that he refused to sign Act No. 150, resulting in his removal from office. (iii) It is mendacious because Atty. Edgar Velastegui Romero, the Secretary, falsely certified that Act No. 150 was unanimously approved on July 4th of 2008. (iv) Act No. 150 dismissed the former General Manager of the AGD and appointed his replacement, Carlos Bravo Macias, a lawyer linked to Juan Falconi Puig, the manifest enemy of the Isaias family, with the clear goal of seizing the Isaias Group's assets.

Carlos Bravo Macias, the new General Manager of the AGD, used Act No. 150 as grounds for his rulings to seize the companies of the Isaias Group on July 9th and subsequently, in spite of the fact that this ruling of the Directors of the AGD allegedly of July 4th of 2008 had additional flaws that hindered it from being applied legitimately. (i) It lacked power, as it did not contain a clear and precise order or mandate to seize the assets of the Isaias family, but instead a general mandate to apply Article 29 of the Law of Economic and Tax Reform; and (ii) It was null and void. It had no legal validity whatsoever due to the lack of the signature of the Minister of Finances, Fausto Ortiz de la Cadena. Both circumstances are the logical and legal consequences of the provisions of Article 22 of the Law of Economic and Tax Reform, which establishes that the Board of Directors is the AGD's governing agency, that the General Manager is merely the executor of the Board, and that the signature of the Minister of Finances is an express legal requirement for a ruling of the AGD's Board of Directors to be valid.

This situation is nothing short of scandalous. The ruling that served as grounds for the seizures is false, is not signed by the principle official commissioned to authorize it and has no legal validity.

6

LA FAMILIA ISAÍAS: TRES GENERACIONES DE EMPRESARIOS

By 2015, exactly a century will have passed since the grandfather of Roberto and William and founder of this clan dedicated to business activities, Emilio Isaias Abi-Hanna, opened his first business in the Ecuadorian town of Catarama. This was the cornerstone of a business empire built on hard work, sacrifice, effort, confidence in its clients and an uncommon entrepreneurial vision, which was passed down from generation to generation.

Without much effort, Roberto recalls many of the stories told by his grandfather, his uncles and his father. From this world of business, which he was compelled to enter prematurely, scenes that left an impact on his life from childhood pass through his memory in rapid succession. We have also availed of biographical information provided by Rodolfo Perez Pimentel in his webpage, as well as newspaper clippings that faithfully reported every interesting detail related to the life of this family of active entrepreneurs.

At the beginning of the 20th Century, Sequiet Eljait, situated in the western mountains of Lebanon, was a small village with only a few families. At that time, it was a poor village where residents cultivated grapes and olives and very few people were landowners. There, in the midst of a peasant family that owned a small farm, Mema Kozhaya Habi-Hanna was born in 1892, later changing his name to Emilio Isaias Abi-Hanna upon his arrival in Ecuador.

In the village, life passed peacefully, almost monotonously, offering few opportunities for its youth, whose only future lay in the agricultural activities of their families. The authorities' persecution of religious minorities, especially Maronite Christians, broke the monotony, forcing many young people to leave Sequiet Eljait.

Emilio was the second of four children from the marriage of Sfein Kozhaya Abi-Hanna and Frisina Taunus, Maronite Christians dedicated to their little farm, where they grew olives, grapes and mulberries for nourishing silkworms.

Emilio attended the school run by his uncle, Hanna Kozhaya, who was the town's only teacher. After finishing this basic education, many youths considered emigrating to Europe or the Americas, as many others had done before them, motivated by the news of those who had prospered and triumphed on American soil.

In addition to the village's poverty, the limited opportunities for young people to have a promising future and the religious persecution, the Turkish draft during the Balkan War heavily influenced the decision of Emilio and other youths to travel to Beirut and board a boat for Europe in 1912.

From Europe, he set sail for America. His plans were to go to Brazil, after stopping in Ecuador to visit his older half-brother, Angel Kozhaya, who was from his father's first marriage. Angel was married to Maria Barquet Abi-Hanna, with whom he had two daughters who died from tropical diseases.

After a crossing that lasted for months, Emilio disembarked at the port of Guayaquil, where he contacted a Lebanese family friend named Gabriel Assaf. His friend suggested a trip to Alausi, where he visited his friends, the Azar brothers. Before returning to Guayaquil, he visited Riobamba, Ambato and Quito by train. This tour allowed him to quickly get to know Ecuador's geography and its most important cities.

On his way back to Guayaquil, he met with another of his friends named Antonio Hanna Tanus, whose commercial operations were headquartered in Vinces. He then left for Catarama, where his brother Angel lived. With the help and advice of his friends and family, he began the odyssey of forging his own destiny.

He began as an agricultural worker, while he saved up some money and overcame the language barrier. After eight months, he became a traveling salesman and made an agreement with his friend, Hanna, as to the zone he would work in the province of Los Rios.

With surprising quickness, he learned everything related to his new profession. He traveled through the Guayas Basin, Catarama, Ventanas and Babahoyo. With his fabrics on his shoulder, he went from home to home in the urban areas and visited the riverside ranches in the rural areas. He carried his merchandise on foot, by mule and over the rivers. This merchandise became increasingly diverse, not only because of the innovations and new products in the market, but also because of the frequent orders placed by his clients. He learned that trust and honor in his work were fundamental for making friends and winning the hearts of peasants.

He overcame the difficulties of the tropics, battling the mosquitoes, snakes and plagues that always stalk those who walk there. He dodged tropical diseases and the harsh winters that caused dangerous floods in the rivers and streams he traveled, often threatening his cargo. After that, he had to withstand the summers with their infernal temperatures. All of these tough experiences tempered his character and provided him with the basic knowledge he would need to embark on his commercial and business ventures.

At the time of the boom in cacao prices, which lasted for over a decade, his savings, along with loans from his brother Angel, helped him to purchase this product from the cacao plantations and send it directly to exporters in Guayaquil.

In this way, he was able to accumulate the necessary capital for his first business venture. In 1915, he opened a grocery store in the municipality of Catarama. Besides fabric, clothing and lace, he also sold basic staples, such as grain, oil, crackers, noodles, etc. A lot of this merchandise was bartered for cacao, which he stored in the back of his shop.

In 1918, he married the widow of his brother Angel, Maria Barquet, with whom he had eight children: six boys (Juan, Estefano, Pedro, Alfredo, Nahim and Enrique) and two girls (Julieta and America). Two of his children were born in Catarama and six in Guayaquil.

In 1923, he decided that he should move to Guayaquil. From this port city, it would be much easier to manage his imports and secure a good education for his children. There, he opened the company EICA (the Spanish initials of the Emilio Isaias Commercial Corporation), which operated in one of the best locations in the city: on the lower floors of the new Government Building in front of the Cathedral at Tenth of August St. and Calle Chimborazo. However, Emilio did not neglect his business in Catarama, where he left his wife's cousin, Ignacio Jorge, in charge of his warehouse and cacao farms, which later became ranches. Each month he visited his businesses in this town, taking orders and bringing merchandise. He regularly took the train inland to visit his clients located in the towns near the railroad. Three years later, he acquired a three-story building located at Olmedo Ave. and Boyaca. He lived with his family on one floor and rented out the other two.

The year 1927 would definitively mark his tendency toward big business. He traveled to Europe to establish contacts, commercial relationships and friendships and there he met providers. Historians relate that those who knew him described him as having remarkable people skills. Emilio had a calm, serene nature and was very courteous. His amiability opened doors for him and earned him friends. In England, he spent three months perfecting what English he knew and took advantage of the opportunity to meet another man of Lebanese descent, Checri Eduen, an important fabric exporter, specializing in cashmere.

The Great Depression of '29 had dire effects on Ecuador's import and export commerce. Exports were not sufficient to generate the currency needed by the import market, currency which was provided through the Central Bank. Considering the bank's inability to acquire dollars or sterling pounds, payments to foreign creditors were halted, along with international credit. Only those who could purchase currency in cash lasted in the market. Small importers closed their businesses, the market was downsized and foreign fabric became more expensive.

Only those with the most lucid minds and the sharpest intelligence were able to turn the crisis into an opportunity. Emilio was already analyzing how to overcome the situation and make the necessary modifications to his import system. While he was in England, his younger brother, Lutfallah, barely 15 years old, arrived in Guayaquil, and at first, wanted to return to Lebanon. However, Lutfallah became part of the solution, as Emilio decided that he should be sent to the city of Kobe in Japan. There, the silk and cashmere industries were highly developed, providing quality as good as in England but at a much lower price. Furthermore, they offered ample credit facilities.

The business did well until the beginning of World War II, due to Japan's participation in it. Lutfallah left for the United States with his wife and son, but just before his departure, he managed to send 50 thousand pieces of linen by boat, which covered almost all of the country's demand for this product between 1942 and 1946.

In May of 1944, Dr. Herman Parker diagnosed Emilio with colon cancer. He traveled to Rochester, New York, and there, the doctors of the Mayo Clinic revised the diagnosis to stomach cancer and successfully operated on him.

After his convalescence, he traveled to New York City and founded the "South and North Corporation," dedicated to the purchase of raw fabric. The office was located at No. 2 Stone Street, near customs and the banking district. It was characteristic of Emilio Isaias to open his offices at strategic locations for sales or customs, or near the financial district, depending on the activity the office would be carrying out.

While he was in New York, he received a welcome visit from his sons, Enrique and Nahim, who were going to study at the Irving School. A college education abroad was one of Emilio's biggest priorities, which he handed down from generation to generation. This, along with his constant trips and those of his family to Japan, Europe, England and the United States, explains the level of modernization and the use of cutting-edge technology that characterized his companies in Ecuador. This was one of the Group's primary contributions to Ecuador's industrial and financial development, a contribution that Emilio made from the very beginning of his business activities. Its effects not only benefited the Group, but also

Ecuadorian industry in general, given that it forced his competitors to modernize, as well.

In 1946, he returned to Ecuador, and the following year began construction on the most modern textile factory in the country. It was named San Vicente and it operated in Quito, where the national textile industry was concentrated. It boasted approximately 950 looms and was dedicated to producing simple cloth, with the goal of capturing the lower- and middle-class market. In 1948, the factory began operations and Juan and Estefano were entrusted with managing it.

Emilio Isaias had a deep appreciation for family, which was not only reflected in the solidarity of the Group, in spite of the fact that each person carried out different activities, but also in the search for the material conditions to bring family members together. The majority of his companies had their headquarters in Guayaquil. In this city, he constructed a comfortable building on the Embankment with a spectacular view of the river and a lovely Andalusian patio in back. He put his son, Enrique, in charge of decorating his apartment on the eighth floor, and the other apartments were occupied by his children. Every Sunday, he met with his children and grandchildren for lunch, and the menu always included the exquisite Arab dishes that his wife carefully prepared for the occasion. Afterwards, Emilio visited the Lebanese Union Society to play cards or dice with his friends and brush up on his Arabic. He also spoke English and Spanish.

FORTIFICATION OF THE GROUP

Emilio's business activities continued without respite. His sons finished their studies abroad and, upon their return, were entrusted with new projects. The family also grew through marriages and grandchildren and everyone became involved in the businesses.

In the 50's, Pedro founded the Canada Dry soft drink factory, and in 1958, acquired all of the shares of La Filantropica Savings, which was experiencing difficulties.

Estefano, in addition to his dedication to textiles, contributed to the Group's diversification by acquiring dealerships for Case tractors, outboard motors and IBM personal computers. Alfredo took charge of the Aztra Sugar Mill and Nahim assumed the administration of La Filantropica upon Estefano's death.

TRAGEDY IN THE LIFE OF THE ISAIAS'

The Isaias family experienced various tragedies, always accepting stoically. Some were random, arising from a tragic fate that revealed itself most of all during the sixties, while others were the result of common criminals and guerilla groups. They threatened the family and its tranquility, and only a deep affection for Ecuador, which had witnessed the growth of the family's home and business, stopped everyone from relocating to another country.

In November of 1960, Pedro Isaias perished in an accident of AREA Airlines, which covered the route from Guayaquil to Quito. He was married to Maria Luisa Bucaram. Besides business activities, Pedro was interested in politics. He had been elected to Congress as the representative of the Galapagos province and was only 38 years old. A short time earlier, Pedro had acquired La Filantropica Savings and his loss was deeply felt.

A few years later, on the night of January 15th of 1965, there was another fateful occurrence. After finishing their workday on EICA, the Isaias brothers met to devote a little time to discussing business and the day's events, as was customary. The door to the warehouse remained open, given the safety of the city where there was little crime. That night, Enrique, Juan and Nahim were there and were surprised by four hooded men, who, in response to Juan's defensive reaction, shot at him and Nahim, who was wounded in the shoulder. Enrique was attacked with a knife and died as a consequence of several wounds.

Tragedy continued to surround the Isaias'. In 1966, around the time of Holy Week, Estefano was returning from Salinas, a small town on the beach, accompanied by Antonio Kozhaya and his brother-in-law, Domingo Simon. The automobile driven by Antonio had a violent collision at kilometer forty of the coast highway and all of the occupants were killed.

In 1967, Juan had to withstand further torture. He was kidnapped in Quito and his captors demanded half a million dollars, which was to be deposited in Bogota. Two persons suspected of belonging to the gang of kidnappers were arrested at the Colombian border and revealed that Juan was being held captive in Cotacallao. Juan was freed by the police, consequentially risking his life, but fortunately, there was a happy ending.

The course of nature also claimed its share. Emilio Isaias, the patriarch, the heart and soul of the business ventures, died of pneumonia in Guayaquil Clinic on June 25th of 1971 at the age of 79. In his wake, he left a trail of success in all of his industrial and commercial endeavors. His teachings were well-assimilated by his sons, grandsons and great grandsons, who continued growing and diversifying the Group. In spite of his low profile, Emilio was widely acknowledged for his generosity, his goodness and his friendly day-to-day manner. His values, his will to overcome obstacles, his natural business abilities and his work ethic were all inherited by his descendants.

The tragic chapter of the family history continued with the kidnapping and subsequent murder of Nahim Isaias Barquet on September 2nd of 1985 in Guayaquil. Nahim was kidnapped by members of the guerilla groups M-19 of Colombia and Alfaro Vive of Ecuador on Wednesday, August 7th of 1985. The kidnappers demanded a million dollars, a plane to take them to Quito, asylum in the Nicaraguan Embassy and the release of members of their groups who were imprisoned in the country, threatening to kill Nahim if their demands were not met. President Leon Febres Cordero considered that these conditions were unacceptable because of the disastrous precedent they would set. The investigations, arrests and raids carried out by the authorities allowed them to discover that the captors had Nahim sequestered in a villa in the La Chala residential complex.

Once they had located the site, the police and members of the Marine Infantry proceeded to surround the area for four blocks and all inhabitants of the zone were evacuated. The President personally directed the rescue operation from Police Headquarters. However, once they learned of the authorities' rescue mission, the kidnappers shot Nahim. He was taken to Guayaquil Clinic where he underwent surgery, but an hour later, he was pronounced dead. All of his captors, three men and one woman, were killed in the rescue operation.

Nahim was the architect of the Isaias Group's continuity, along with his nephews, Roberto, William and Estefano. As a banker, he exercised the duties of Filanbanco's General Manager, the Honorary President of the Republic National Bank of Miami and President of Seguros Rocafuerte. As a diplomat, he carried out duties as the Honorary General Consul of the Dominican Republic, and on two occasions as the Deacon of the Guayaquil Diplomatic Corps. He also created the Isaias Foundation, through which he cultivated his philanthropic spirit.

NAHIM AND ROBERTO: DIVERSIFICATION AND CONSOLIDATION OF THE GROUP

La The Isaias family remained united in spite of the tragedies. During his life, Emilio had not only delegated responsibilities, but had also distributed ownership of the companies fairly and equitably among his children and grandchildren, who had received training in industry and commerce abroad. In time, due to life events, each family group decided to go its own way, some of them moving to the United States.

However, Nahim and his nephews, Roberto, William and Estefano Jr., continued running the family business together. All three were Estefano's sons, and Nahim took responsibility for their education when his brother passed away.

Nahim initiated and guided Roberto in the knowledge of all banking activity to the point where, upon his uncle's death, Roberto assumed the directorship of Filanbanco and leadership of the Group, and was instrumental in the successful development of the Republic National Bank of Miami. Roberto remembers Nahim as follows: "My Uncle Nahim was the one who most liked to invest in different businesses. He was the driving force for diversification and investments outside of Ecuador. The others were much more conservative, more peaceful and less aggressive in business. They had to be sure of a business' good prospects before making investments. In this way, they were a lot like my grandfather, who took the same approach."

"My Uncle Nahim had an excellent nose for business and a great social sensibility. He always considered the social areas where he could provide assistance through his businesses. Perhaps I was infected by the aggressiveness he had for business. So, I believe that I inherited the aggressiveness from my uncle and my negotiation skills from my grandfather."

"Whenever we arrived at negotiations, my uncle left me in charge of them. I believe that it was an innate condition; the university could provide me with the means to manage a company, but did not give me the capacity or the ability to negotiate; that is something one is born with. I believe that it is in the genes. In each family, there are those who enjoy the industrial aspect, the commercial aspect or the administrative aspect of business."

Roberto was educated in the United States, along with most of his cousins. He attended the Philadelphia College of Textiles & Science, where he earned a degree in Textile Administration and Marketing. He consolidated and modernized the companies in the areas of agroindustry, finances and textiles and increased diversification by adding new companies. Roberto recalls the early diversification of the Isaias Group: "The first few years of the brewery coincided with the pricing problems arising from the currency devaluation, and we decided to sell off 80% of the company to the Brazilians of Brahma Beer and subsequently sold them the remaining 20%. We then made incursions into the petroleum industry, and also into the agricultural sector during the 80's, which was the decade when we made the most investments. The textile industry was not yet the most important one, because it had been additionally affected by the import of these products from China."

"In most cases, we founded our own companies. In other cases, we formed partnerships. In

1970, for example, we were associated with a TV channel, and from that point, we began to enter the communications business. We also entered the cable business around the year '85 or '86, with another partner."

"Our expansion into communications continued and we managed to form partnerships with Motorola and Skype. By this time, things were much easier for us, not only because we traveled a lot, but also because we had already bought the Republic National Bank in Miami in 1970. People knew who we were and foreign firms sought us out to associate and invest with us in the market. So, we continued growing. However, some companies were not successful. For example, the brewery never got off the ground because of the economic climate of the devaluation, which increased the cost of importing barley and the cost of the bottles. Another company in which we made an incursion without good results was in the area of banana exports. We lost a lot of money. Bananas were subject to a fixed price in Ecuador, rather than the international price, which was variable. So, when the price went down abroad, we had to assume the loss."

The Isaias Group under Roberto's direction is today one of Ecuador's largest and most diversified business groups, in spite of the seizure of more than 150 of its companies on the part of

Correa's government. The Isaias' have interests in numerous sectors, including telecommunications, media, industry, distribution, vehicle promotion and assembly, agriculture, mining, petroleum, port services, general insurance and life insurance.

In developing its plans for expansion and diversification, the Group maintains permanent management of the design and execution of new business ventures, seeking to increase its active participation in new areas of national and international business, either directly or through partnerships and strategic alliances, by taking advantage of the existing capacities and talents of its current companies and human resources.

The Group operates joint ventures in the following areas:

- Media (free-to-air television, cable television, Internet, radio, magazines)
- Import and promotion of automobiles, motors, construction equipment, commercial vehicles, heavy equipment
- Agroindustry, the food industry, the textile industry, the tuna industry, graphics and printing, cardboard containers, promotion and distribution of consumables, farming and agriculture, sugarcane farming and sugar processing and promotion

- Real estate development focused on low income urban developments in various cities in the country, as well urban development.
- Specialized mail
- Tourism and hotels
- Mining investments – precious metals, exploration and mining of hydrocarbons
- Agriculture, African oil palms, bananas, sugarcane, livestock, vehicle rentals, tuna fishing, processing and promotion of edible oils, shrimp fisheries and port operations

The Group's Mission has always been focused on leadership in the sectors it manages, geared toward the satisfaction of consumer needs and committed to contributing to the country's socioeconomic development in a sustainable way. One constant throughout the Group's history has been its active contribution to social assistance programs.

There has been no lack of public recognition and decoration for Roberto's services to his country. Like his grandfather, Emilio, and his Uncle Nahim, the most outstanding for his business achievements, Roberto has also distinguished himself by his accomplishments. In a daring financial transaction, he succeeded in acquiring the Aztra Sugar Mill, now known as La Troncal and considered to be the Group's crowning achievement. Unfortunately, the sugar mill was yet another victim of the government's illegal seizures.

145

7

THE NAHIM ISAIAS FOUNDATION: THE GROUP'S SOCIAL RESPONSIBILITY

The Isaias' contributions to Ecuador through their companies have gone far beyond providing employment for thousands of people, advancing the country's technological development through the use of cutting-edge technologies in all of the Group's economic and financial activities and establishing the shrimp and banana companies' presence in the international market through investments and the financial support of Filanbanco.

The Group's social responsibility and commitment to the country's wellbeing, especially in the case of the poorest people within the companies' areas of operations, have gone on for decades. Through all of its members, the family has demonstrated its generosity from the very beginning. Roberto tells us: "The family was always very involved in the social aspect and we provided assistance in many different projects. First, we decided to support the training of educators. So, we called the professors, based on our conviction that, if our professors were not well-educated and well-trained, they would not be in a position to provide a good education to their students. So, we began to create a type of fund so that profes-

147

sors could specialize in the disciplines they taught. Together with the association of professors in service to the State, we managed to create an interesting program and also a social security fund, which they administered. This was during the 80's and those funds still exist and have served to finance housing. However, the training programs could not continue. Some Ministers did not think that it was a good idea for our organization to be involved in supporting this type of program. Unfortunately, in some cases, we had to cut off our support, but we have always felt that education is a very important sector for the development of any country, especially in Latin America.

The Isaias family's support of various social causes was channeled and institutionalized by the Isaias Barquet brothers on October 20th of 1967, when they created the La Filantropica Foundation. On that day, there was a meeting of the Isaias Barquet brothers, Emilio, Juan, Nahim and Alfredo, the Isaias Dassum brothers, William and Roberto, and other persons close to the family, such as Jose Barakat, Maria Lucia de Simon, Maria Luisa Bucaram de Isaias and Carlos Guzman Aguirre, in his capacity as manager of Banco La Filantropica. Their main objective was to contribute financially to the performance of charity work, and in particular, to contribute toward the education of children and adults in a vocation that would allow them and their families to improve their position. In addition to the various contributions originating from the companies, it was agreed that the rent generated from the house located on the corner of Chimborazo and Garcia Goyena would be allocated for sustaining the Foundation.

Later, on July 21st of 1988, the La Filantropica Foundation changed its trade name to the Filanbanco Foundation, which was later named "The Nahim Isaias Foundation", in memory of the philanthropist, Nahim Isaias, and his desire to carry out a unified and transcendent effort in benefit of the most needy.

This non-profit organization targeted its valuable contributions toward vital areas, such as health, education, culture and the athletic training of thousands of the country's children and teens. Roberto recalls that the Foundation began its work in health programs with the adaptation of two spaces that were converted into small doctor's offices, each one fully equipped and staffed with a doctor and a nurse. They were set up in the community areas of Guayaquil and Quito.

In a short time, the project was expanded with twenty more doctor's offices with the same characteristics, distributed in strategic locations in various cities, such as Cuenca, Portoviejo, Manta, Riobama, Ambato, Machala, Esmeraldas, El Triunfo, Santo Domingo, La Troncal, Ibarra, Guaranda, Anconcito, Milagro, Jipijapa and Azogues, providing approximately one hundred thousand medical consultations per year. Since 1988, these offices have provided uninterrupted medical care, performing silent but effective social assistance that is definitely transcendental.

The Foundation and healthcare: In June of 1997, the first Filansalud Comprehensive Healthcare Center was opened in Guasmo Sur, in cooperation with the Catholic University of Guayaquil. Through this program, the Foundation initiated a comprehensive project, offering a pharmacy and services in general medicine, pediatrics, gynecology, laboratory analysis, odontology, dermatology and echosonagraphy, among others, all at very affordable prices. Six months later, the Medical Brigades were established in order to help the people affected by the consequences of the El Niño phenomenon. The populations of the provinces of Guayas, Los Rios, Esmeraldas, El Oro and Manabi received treatment and medication. This was managed by groups of volunteers made up of employees from different branches of Filanbanco and external philanthropists, who managed to care for more than 15,000 affected people through their united efforts.

The Foundation carried out care and motivation programs, like Early Stimulation for children up to four years old, children's health programs and their respective immunization campaigns, and women's support groups for pregnancy, menopause and prevention of uterine cancer. Likewise, patients were educated through monthly presentations on prevention of seasonal illnesses, AIDS and STD's.

Conceived on the fundamental values of the human being and the family as the backbone of society, the Foundation created the "Uniting Ties of Love" project, which consisted of raising the awareness of couples, under the premise that "the marriages that last are not those that have never had conflicts, but rather those in which the conflicts have served a useful purpose." The goal of this program was reached in November of 1998, with the legal marriage of 51 couples of limited financial means, who had children within a common law marriage. These couples were involved in many of the Foundation's activities over the following 10 years.

The Foundation's seriousness, dedication, timely services and coverage allowed it to qualify for auctions of the resources of the Ministry of Social Wellbeing and the Pan-American Development Bank in the year 2001. At that time, the "Growing with Our Children" program was established, beginning with care for children under five. Today this program covers 1,020 children located in high-risk areas in the cities of Guayaquil and Babahoyo.

In keeping with the alleviation of suffering from disease, the Foundation created the Specialized Medical Center. It opened on August 14th of 2003 and currently cares for approximately 14,000 patients per month, through a group made up of 49 doctors, 8 administrators, 3 assistants and 2 general service support technicians. It provides care in 24 specialties, as well as laboratory, echogram, Pap smear and pharmacy services, among others.

In addition to these activities, there were prevention campaigns for fatty liver, prostate problems and osteoporosis, a parasite cleansing campaign for children and adults and other campaigns developed within the organization against asthma and the organization against diabetes.

Healthcare really makes a significant impact on the poor population. Management reports show that, in 2009, 322,343 patients were seen, of which 10% received pediatric services, 8% received gynecological services and the rest received various specialized services. As of May of 2010, the Foundation was caring for an average of 1,250 patients per day.

We should also recognize the Foundation's efforts in the weekly distribution of 80,000 rations of snacks in orphanages, convalescent hospitals, public hospitals, public cafeterias, schools, etc. The snacks consist of, milk, chocolate milk, cream cheese, custard and juices.

The Nahim Isaias Foundation has cooperative agreements with State institutions, universities, companies and municipalities, which facilitate its work and increase the impact of its programs on the target populations.

The Nahim Isaias Museum, Guayaquil: Founded in July of 1989, this museum contains the most important collection of Colonial Art from the Quiteña School. Thousands of works make up this collection. The museum is part of the Filanbanco Foundation, whose sole objective is to disseminate and promote culture in benefit of the community. Each year a varied and extensive cultural program is presented, including seminars, workshops, conferences, poetry readings, classical music recitals, theatre, painting and sculpture exhibits and book presentations.

Meriting special mention is the creation of the exhibition area for an extraordinary collection of pieces from the pre-Hispanic culture of the Ecuadorian coast on the first floor of the Museum, which was opened to the public on July 20th of 1996, where 3,200 pieces are exhibited in 15 displays.

Filanbanco Museum in Quito: This museum contains one of the most complete collections of Ecuadorian art from the 16th through the 19th

Centuries, four hundred years of evolution during which one can appreciate the shift from Baroque art, after the conquest, to the religious iconography of the past century. The works are on permanent display. The museum also mounts expositions of contemporary art by national and foreign artists.

The Foundation and Culture: The community contributions of the Filanbanco Foundation have also been geared toward cultural activities through the art gallery, the traditional National Chorus Festivals and the Youth Chamber Orchestra.

The Filanbanco Gallery of Art is the most visited in Guayaquil, with an estimated seventy thousand people discovering the message of each artist or painter that exhibits his or her work. Those invited to the inaugurations have included notable personalities from the Ecuadorian cultural and intellectual world, poets, journalists and the full gamut of talented individuals who help make life more gracious and inspirational for the museum's visitors.

The National Chorus Festivals, in homage to the Guayaquil Foundation, have served to bring together the best choruses from diverse cities in Ecuador, bringing with them the enthusiastic message of their interpretations.

The Filanbanco Youth Chamber Orchestra marked a tendency toward good music, which has lent great prestige to the Foundation's cultural mission. Thanks to the work of its members, the seedbed of national artists has been fortified, contributing to the reinforcement and prestige of many other groups and orchestras in the country.

Education: The Filanbanco Foundation contributes to education through agreements and donations, in addition to promoting, sponsoring and developing technical-professional training programs. In collaboration with the Catholic University and the Esquel Ecuador Foundation, the book, "The conquest of intelligence" was published with the goal of supporting the physical and mental development of the marginal urban child population, and the Foundation made another positive contribution by adapting and constructing educational centers for low-income children.

8

THE ALLEGED BANK EMBEZZLEMENT: THE JURISTS' ANALYSIS

The Isaias' were not public officials, nor did they manage State resources so as to have committed embezzlement

The negative effects of the economic crisis experienced in Ecuador in 1998 on the banking sector were so evident and so clear that any economic, political or legal analyst must use it as a context without which it would be impossible to understand the Filanbanco Case. The following events set the stage upon which Filanbanco's crisis would unfold, as already discussed in previous chapters, but which is valid as a preamble to the legal analysis if one wishes to discredit the widely-disseminated myth that Filanbanco caused Ecuador's economic crisis of 1998-1999.

The General Manager of the Central Bank of Ecuador, economist Miguel Davila Castillo, informed the Attorney General of the country's economic outlook in 1998, characterized by deterioration of the fiscal situation, aggravated by the fall in petroleum export prices and a reduction in external sources of financing for the country, a result of the international financial turbulence of the time. The economic indicators in 1998, which Mr. Davila made known to the Attorney General, demonstrated the magnitude of the crisis. Annual inflation was at 43.4%, the monetary reserve was reduced by 255.2 million dollars, placing it at 1,698.3 million on December 31st 1998, and growth in the GNP for 1998 was only 0.4% compared to 1997, attributable primarily to the devastating effects of the El Niño phenomenon.

So, it can be concluded that the Filanbanco crisis arose from the interaction of various factors beyond the scope and will of the bank's shareholders and administrators, as stated by Walter Guerrero Vivanco, who will be extensively quoted in this chapter. The El Niño phenomenon was one of the most significant causes of the crisis, given that the financial entities that had granted the highest volume of credit in the coastal region of Ecuador were the most affected by it, as was the case with Filanbanco, and in any event, the problem was a generalized financial crisis and not the mismanagement of a banking institution. The jurists performed their analysis in this context, as well, and here we will point out the most important input regarding the alleged "embezzlement" from a legal standpoint, provided by Guerrero Vivanco and Larrea Holguin.

DEFINITION OF THE MATTER

The legal analysis regarding Case No. 57-2000 against the ex-shareholders of Filanbanco, Roberto and William Isaias, centers on the accusation of bank embezzlement.

Bank embezzlement, which is the object of this trial, refers to the supposed misuse of funds loaned by the Central Bank of Ecuador to Filanbanco during the period between September 24th and December 2nd of 1998, as shown both in the Order Setting the Matter for Trial and the Summons to Plenary Action. During that time, the administrators of Filanbanco would have had to act intentionally, causing damages to the Central Bank by misusing the money it provided to Filanbanco in a line of credit in order to resolve the bank's liquidity problems.

THE FACTS

As the economic and financial situation in Ecuador and the banking system at the time of the events is already well-known, we will not make further reference to it. However, it is clear that this situation had negative repercussions for Filanbanco, which, in 1998, had more than three hundred thousand accountholders, both individuals and legal entities, some of which managed large volumes of money and affected the economic lives of hundreds of thousands of other people.

As such, no one can deny that insolvency on the part of Filanbanco would have done great harm to a large portion of Ecuador's economically active population and to the prestige of the Ecuadorian State. That was the motivation that led the financial authorities to seek means of avoiding this serious problem to the greatest possible extent and to establish liquidity credit.

THE LEGAL GROUNDS FOR GRANTING LIQUIDITY CREDIT

The Central Bank of Ecuador authorized to extend liquidity loans to Filanbanco and other financial entities, based on express constitutional and legal regulations.

Article 24 of the Law on Monetary Procedure and the State Bank, in effect since 1994, allowed the Monetary Board, in cases of a lack of liquidity in institutions under the control of the Superintendence of Banks, to authorize the Central Bank to grant credit for a maximum term of sixty days, collateralized by qualifying documents or endorsed portfolio documents. Between 1994 and 1995, the Central Bank of Ecuador granted credit to several financial institutions, applying the previously mentioned legal regulations, and based on that experience, established its Treasury Operations. This preventive mechanism in the face of consequential withdrawal crises made it possible to open a line of credit, in which the Central Bank had to grant the financial institution one or more loans on each date that they were requested, as long as they were in compliance with the established requirements.

In the Treasury Operations Agreement, it was established that the "mutual contract" between the Bank and the financial institution entered into effect each time there was a payout. As such, it was a mutual contract of a civil, rather than a penal nature. Furthermore, once the contract was signed, Filanbanco was actually the **owner of the funds**, in accordance with the provisions of the Civil Code and the Code of Commerce, and was obligated to pay back the same amount as it received, plus the agreed-upon interest. As the owner, Filanbanco would avail of this money; however, given the unusual situation being experienced in the country, and due to the goal being pursued, which was to avoid serious damages to thousands and thousands of people and the entire national economy, a series of restrictions were established, such as the prohibition on granting new loans while the previous ones were still unpaid (to the Central Bank) and the agreement that Filanbanco would not grant new loans to its clients, either. These restrictions were rigorously enforced and, although they did not invalidate the mutual character of the loan, they signified a serious decrease in the power that a borrower would normally have to avail of those resources.

The new Political Constitution of the Republic, which went into effect on August 10th of 1998, ratified the full validity of the previously adopted legal provisions, establishing that, "...until the State has the sufficient legal resources to confront financial crises, and for a term no greater than two years from the effective date of this Constitution, the Central Bank of Ecuador may grant stability and solvency credit to financial institutions..."

The Central Bank approved Filanbanco for a line of credit in the amount of 972 billion sucres on September 18th of 1998, but at that time, the bank only required 290 billion sucres, the equivalent of 423 million dollars.

With regard to the collateral required of Filanbanco for approval of the liquidity credit, the General Manager of the Central Bank of Ecuador informed the Attorney General, through Official Communiqué SE-1462-2000-01867 of June 12th of 2000, that the Central Bank of Ecuador granted the liquidity and stability credit to Filanbanco, based on "sufficient collateral; in this sense, the Central Bank has carefully ensured that the credit facilities granted to all those financial institutions requiring them are backed with qualified or appraised collateral that would allow for recuperation of the awarded credit in the event that it is not paid off in a timely manner." The General Manager also added that, "...the amount of credit granted to Filanbanco was at all times backed by collateral valued at 120% of that amount, and this information was sent to the Attorney General through Official Communiqué SE-2556-99 of August 5th of 1999."

THE HIGH INTEREST ON THE LIQUIDITY CREDIT

Although the authorized credit remained in the Central Bank's possession until the time that Filanbanco made payments to its creditors, the Central Bank charged interest determined by the institution, according to the economic conditions of the moment. This interest rose to 120%, adding the enormous figure of approximately a trillion sucres, which is over a million dollars per day. Of the 423 million dollars from the line of credit, only 350 million was used, as approximately 73 million was paid off early. This amount would have constituted a tremendous usury if it were not for the increasing devaluation of the currency: the Central Bank protected its capital by charging such interest, which was in excess of that formally permitted by law, in an effort to offset the daily decrease in the currency's value. This devaluation phenomenon, never before seen in Ecuador, was accentuated by the Central Bank's issuance of fiat currency. This circumstance explains why none of the Bank's authorities, not the Superintendence nor the Executive Branch nor the Legislative Branch objected to the colossal interest charged by the Central Bank. For Filanbanco, the payment of such elevated levels of interest was an unsustainable situation, which accelerated the forfeiture of the bank to the Ecuadorian government.

THE LIQUIDITY CREDIT WAS NOT IN FILANBANCO'S POSSESSION

The controlled management of the liquidity credit by the Central Bank was so rigorous that it could be said that it was not really in Filanbanco's possession. This is a fundamental element when it comes to demonstrating the transparency with which such resources were administered and to dismissing Falconi's treacherous accusations of their corrupt management. The Central Bank, in order to safeguard the recuperation of the resources awarded to Filanbanco, established that the credit granted to cover the necessary reserves was not a resource at the free disposal of the borrowing entity, but rather it was maintained in a collateralized account at the BCE with an automated debit authorization for its payment upon expiration of the term. It also established offsite controls that were applied to all of the borrowing institutions, tracking liquid assets at the balance level.

In order to effectuate payments to foreign banks, it was necessary for Filanbanco to purchase currency from the Central Bank. The withdrawals of accountholders' funds at the teller window or through checks were also regulated by the BCE.

So, it is completely unfounded that the Group made itself rich from the liquidity credit, as the Isaias' enemies proclaim, and much less that it arbitrarily availed of public or private funds, thereby committing embezzlement. The credit was used to cover withdrawals by accountholders and to pay contingency transactions, labor costs and debt service, transactions that were permitted by the current regulations.

THE CHIEF PROSECUTOR OF THE NATION: THERE IS NO EMBEZZLEMENT

After three years of preliminary investigations, the Chief Prosecutor of the Nation recognized and declared that there was no embezzlement. "Although it is true that the formal audit mentions that the funds granted by the Central Bank to Filanbanco, S.A. were used to perform new credit transactions with companies belonging to the same group, it is no less true that, in the reports of economist Miguel Davila Castillo, in his capacity as Manager of the Central Bank, Juan Franco Porras and Antonio Beharano Trujillo, the Managers of Filanbanco, there was no evidence of misuse of public funds originating from the Central Bank of Ecuador and therefore, no embezzlement. As a consequence, it is not possible to sustain the original criterion of the District Attorney, and moreover, because the authorization of credit to affiliated companies was typified as embezzlement subsequent to the actions that gave rise to this process, through Law No. 99-26 published in Official Registry No. 190 of May 13th of 1999, which adds Article 257A to Article 257 of the Penal Code..."

It was the Chief Prosecutor of the Nation who declared that there was no embezzlement. However, for the Group's political enemies, this was not valid and it was necessary to continue this diabolical and devious process to do as much moral and financial harm as possible to the Isaias'.

9
THE LEGAL SITUATION
TEN YEARS LATER

More than a decade has not been sufficient time to conclude the "Filanbanco Case." There are no signs that the political persecution and meddling of the Executive and Legislative Branches in the Judicial Branch in detriment to the Isaias Group will cease, and as such, there will be no other will than that expressed by President Rafael Correa after ordering the seizure of the Isaias' assets in a speech given before the Constituent Assembly for purposes of approving Mandate No. 13 of July 9th of 2008. Correa stated: "Now will come the trials of the Isaias', the persecution of the Isaias', lifelong persecution."

After the lawsuit filed by the Deposit Guarantee Agency in April of 2009 with the State of Florida, requesting a freeze on 20 million dollars in assets of the Isaias Group in Miami, and the countersuit filed by the Isaias brothers' defense, little has happened to change the course of the process.

On May 12th of 2009, the First Chamber of Penal Matters of the National Court of Justice ratified the March 2003 summons to a full trial against the former owners of Filanbanco and eleven other officials for the crime of bank embezzlement. Subsequently, on July 28th of 2009, the lawyers of the brothers, Roberto and William Isaias, filed a motion for extraordinary protection in the Constitutional Court in order to dismiss the criminal accusation of embezzlement, due to the implied unconstitutionality of charging a person retroactively with laws enacted after the fact.

The unwavering will of the Isaias Group to arrive at a definitive resolution in the specific case of the seized companies is expressed in the proposal contained in the communiqué of March 25th of 2010, addressed to President Rafael Correa by the lawyer representing the Isaias brothers, Xavier Castro.

Because we consider this communication to be of great importance, we have decided to transcribe it in its entirety:

Mr. President:

Twenty months ago a seizure of assets was executed against the former share-holders of Filanbanco and also extended to third parties. The grounds for this was a report from the firm Deloitte & Touche (D&T) in which, under an agreed procedure and not an Audit Report, a risk evaluation was made of Filanbanco's assets as of December of 1998, the time that the Isaias family ceased to be a shareholder in the bank.

In the above mentioned report by D&T is a description of the portfolio and other assets, evaluating their risk of recovery, with names, last names and accounts. With the passage of time, as you must have noticed, those assets considered to be unrecoverable could not be more than or other than those that had been determined by the auditing firm. They could be less if, for example, a debtor considered to be uncollectable had paid.

With regard to the legal recourses we are taking against the seizures because Article 29 of the AGD Law is a reform made subsequent to 1998, because Filanbanco was not an AGD bank, but rather of the Ministry of Finances, which is outside the scope of said law, and because the seizure envisaged in Article 29 refers to cases in which there are **liabilities (accountholders) and not unpaid assets (the bank's debtors),** like those described in the D&T report, a few days after the seizure, we **clearly proposed our will to purchase the assets de-**

169

scribed in the report, for which it needed to be updated as to which of those assets had been recovered.

The Banking Board authorized the update of the report, in which the total, under no circumstances could be greater than that which was originally established, as those assets, as of December of 1998, were the only ones considered to be unrecoverable by D&T. The update was not complicated. The procedure was very simple: it was necessary to take the list of described debtors and verify whether they had paid by 2008 or not. If they did not pay, it is fitting to acknowledge the accuracy of the provisional estimate made by D&T. If they did pay, that sum had to be subtracted from the mathematical results in the report. Likewise, this had to be done with the other asset accounts in order to know if the D&T's estimate in 1998 still held in 2008.

At the end of December of 2009, having passed 17 months since the seizure without any notification to the ex-shareholders, the press reported that the liquidator at the time pre-

170

sented a detailed report of all of Filanbanco's portfolio that had not been recovered as of 2009, causing confusion, basically because of two considerations: **Firstly, because the D&T report was not used to update the figures (at-risk portfolio as of 1998), but rather Filanbanco's current portfolio was used, in an attempt to hold us responsible not for what occurred up to December of 1998, but instead up to 2009; and secondly, because the update excluded the other asset accounts that have suffered substantial modification over 11 years.**

On repeated occasions, we have asked to meet with the authorities involved in this case. Their office, sensitive to the situation, on two occasions has stated that the Superintendent of Banks would meet with us, yet we have not gotten an appointment with her in spite of our requests. With the exception of the Citizen Review Panel, no one has paid attention to us or listened to us for over a year, until March 18th of 2010, when we met with the Minister of Finances, to whom the entire file that belonged

171

to the AGD had just been sent, for which reason she was not in a position to receive our defense, much less initiate a process for concluding this matter.

Notwithstanding these considerations, the sale of the seized companies was announced. The AGD declared that these were already their property, and as such, part of their assets. Nevertheless, we continue to be considered as "debtors," that is, a collection account of the AGD. This institution, which is now subrogated to the Ministry of Finances, thus has duplicate assets. If the companies already belong to the State, then their value must be credited to the ex-shareholders as of the date of the seizure (1998). This has not been done. **They consider the assets to be property of the State, and at the same time, they consider the former shareholders to be debtors.**

Furthermore, they have announced that the proceeds from the sale of the companies (and not their fair appraisal value) will be applied to what they refer to as the Isaias' debt. **Thus, it**

is intended to hold us responsible for the companies' loss of value over the past 20 months under the administration of the AGD and the AGD/CFN Trust without any accountability whatsoever. We have not been informed of the profits, nor notified of the appraisal, nor do we know what methodology was used. In fact, the CFN's web page states that the appraisals are confidential and that "interested parties must submit their offers based on the information they have at hand."

As if this were not enough, it has been announced that all of the assets and documental collateral of Filanbanco was transferred to the BCE, without considering that such assets, basically uncollected portfolio, upon having been paid with the assets of the Isaias family, would belong to the family. **The transfer of the documents, furthermore, could easily eliminate every vestige of what occurred during the State administration between the years 1998 and 2009.**

These facts, which are the responsibility of those who are executing this process, Mr. President, do not correspond to the transparency and verticality with which you brand your management of the government.

Our proposal is simple and clear: **to update the value in the D&T report in a transparent manner, and for us to assume the value of those uncollected assets immediately, dismissing any trial or claim to the companies that the State should choose to receive in its fair appraisal. With this will come the definitive resolution of this matter that preoccupies the entire community, and the State will be able to fulfill its promise of putting the means of production into the hands of the community and the workers, free from legal encumbrances.**

I ask, in the most self-restrained manner, that you be willing to hear us, and if possible, that you grant us an appointment to resolve this matter immediately.

Sincerely,
Xavier Castro Munoz

EPILOGUE

A string of violations of human rights from the beginning up to the present, as this matter has not yet ended, is the fundamental characteristic of the persecution against Roberto and William Isaias Dassum, the former President and Vice-President of Filanbanco, respectively.

Only under a dense mantle of official corruption, despicable political interests and a government that criminalizes success can one understand so many violations of the rights of those who have been at the head of a business group that contributed, from the beginnings of the 20th Century and for three subsequent generations, employment and economic growth to Ecuador and that has continued to be burdened by government obstacles.

All of the Isaias' individual liberties and fundamental rights envisaged in various agreements have been violated, including those envisaged in the Universal Declaration of Human Rights, those which were signed by the American States in the American Convention on Human Rights in San Jose, Costa Rica on November 22nd of 1969, those that are enshrined in the Charter of the Organization of the American States and those that are recognized in the American Declaration of Human Rights and Duties. Additionally, basic principles enshrined in the Ecuadorian Constitution were violated.

Political persecution has been ever present in the process from the beginning. The American Convention on Human Rights establishes the Principle of Legality and Retroactivity in Article 9, which states that, "No one may be condemned for actions or omissions that, at the time of their commission, were not criminalized under applicable laws." Roberto and William Isaias Dassum were accused of having committed "bank embezzlement" between September 14th and December 2nd of 1998. However, not only is there no evidence of embezzlement, but also this crime was not typified in the Ecuadorian Penal Code, in which embezzlement only applied to those in public service, which the Isaias brothers never were. Likewise, there have been violations of both the 1998 version of the Constitution of the Republic and the 2008 Montecristi version, which is still in effect. Both constitutions establish that no one may be judged for an act or omission that, at the time of its occurrence, was not typified and punishable under criminal law. This is a case of an accusation with no legal grounds, which violates the universal principle of "*nullum crimen, nulla peona sine lege*" (without law, there is neither crime nor punishment).

This false charge initiated a grave injustice and a political vendetta without respite, which has been revealed in the previous pages of this book. The constitutional guarantees of the presumption of innocence, of due process, of an impartial judge and of the right to defend oneself have all been violated.

There were no legal grounds whatsoever for the seizure of the Isaias brothers' assets effectuated through Ruling AGD-UIO-2008-12 of the Deposit Guarantee Agency (AGD) on July 8th of 2008. It was an act of undue appropriation of another's assets, which the government has been using to its advantage, as occurred with the two television channels with the largest audience in Ecuador, which were put to its use for the campaign for the "yes" vote on the referendum on a Constituent Assembly in order to transform State structures and adapt them to the "Socialism of the 21st Century" project, which has extraordinary similitude to certain cases in Venezuela.

No country that deems itself to be a lawful State or claims to respect the fundamental rights of its citizens can do what the Constituent Assembly did through Mandate No. 13 in the name of the people. This mandate completely suppressed the Isaias' right to defense in Ecuador.

The Constituent Assembly's Mandate No. 13 of July 9th of 2008 legitimized the illegal actions of the General Manager of the Deposit Guarantee Agency when he seized the assets of the Isaias family.

177

The seizures were carried out without any prior analysis or legal ruling on the financial liability of Roberto and William Isaias (much less criminal liability, as the process has not been concluded), that is, there were no legal grounds for carrying them out; there was no prior expropriation or appraisal of the assets, as stipulated in the Constitution. Basically, in addition to legalizing an illegal seizure of assets without valid justification, the Mandate violated the right to defense on the part of the affected parties because the Constituent Assembly ordered that no legal authority could hear petitions or motions for constitutional protection or control filed by the entrepreneurs, thus stripping them of their fundamental right to representation and legal recourse through some type of administrative or judicial appeal of the seizure.

In exile, Roberto and William Isaias continue being victims of the judicial excesses of this process. They hope that one day the politicization of justice will cease in Ecuador, that their honor and assets will be restored and that once again they will be able to create wealth in their country and contribute to its development.

APPENDICES

0032664

RAFAEL CORREA DELGADO

PRESIDENTE CONSTITUCIONAL DE LA REPÚBLICA

CONSIDERANDO:

Que mediante Decreto Ejecutivo 2084-A, publicado en el Registro Oficial 537 de 29 de septiembre de 1994, se promulgó el Reglamento a la Ley de Documentos de Viaje;

Que todo ecuatoriano tiene derecho a obtener un pasaporte para salir del territorio nacional y movilizarse en el exterior;

Que no obstante gozar del derecho supradicho, cuando un ecuatoriano es acusado o condenado por el cometimiento de delitos comunes, el uso del pasaporte como medio para evadir su captura, resultaría ilegítimo e impediría la realización de la justicia;

Que es necesario que el Ministerio de Relaciones Exteriores, Comercio e Integración, sus dependencias y Oficinas Consulares se abstengan de otorgar pasaporte a los ecuatorianos que se hallaren prófugos de la justicia, para evitar su evasión;

Que el segundo inciso del artículo 5 de la Codificación de la Ley de Documentos de Viaje establece que la concesión de pasaporte se hará de acuerdo a la Ley y su Reglamento; y,

En uso de las atribuciones conferidas por el artículo 171, numeral 5 de la Constitución Política de la República;

DECRETA:

Expedir la siguiente reforma al REGLAMENTO A LA LEY DE DOCUMENTOS DE VIAJE

Art. 1.- Agréguese el siguiente artículo a continuación del Artículo 41:

"Art. 41.1- El Ministerio de Relaciones Exteriores, sus dependencias y Oficinas Consulares se abstendrán de otorgar pasaporte a los ecuatorianos que se hallaren prófugos de la justicia.

Para el efecto, el Ministerio de Gobierno y Policía enviará periódicamente al Ministerio de Relaciones Exteriores, Comercio e Integración una lista que contenga los nombres, número de cédula de ciudadanía, copia de las órdenes judiciales y otros datos para

0002665

RAFAEL CORREA DELGADO

PRESIDENTE CONSTITUCIONAL DE LA REPÚBLICA

facilitar la identificación de aquellos ciudadanos ecuatorianos que se hallaren prófugos de la justicia.

Art. 2.- De la ejecución del presente Decreto Ejecutivo, que entrará en vigencia a partir de su publicación en el Registro Oficial, encárguese a la Ministra de Relaciones Exteriores, Comercio e Integración.

Dado en el Palacio Nacional, en Quito a   14 de febrero de 2008

Rafael Correa Delgado
PRESIDENTE CONSTITUCIONAL DE LA REPÚBLICA

María Isabel Salvador Crespo,
MINISTRA DE RELACIONES EXTERIORES,
COMERCIO E INTEGRACIÓN,

181

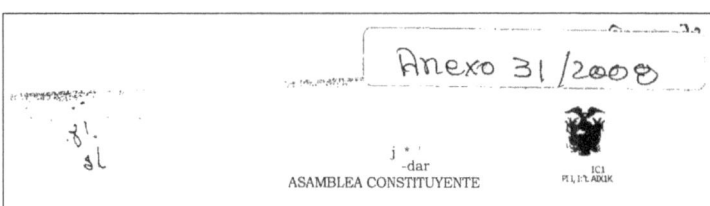

j * '
-dar
ASAMBLEA CONSTITUYENTE

Ciudad Alfaro, Montecristi, julio 9 de 2008

Señor Arquitecto
Fernando Cordero
PRESIDENTE DE LA ASAMBLEA CONSTITUYENTE
Presente.

De nuestra consideración:

La resolución expedida por el Gerente General de la Agencia de Garantía de Depósitos, mediante la cual se procedió a la incautación de las empresas del grupo económico Isaías, exige la toma de decisiones por parte de la Asamblea Constituyente que permitan, por una parte; garantizar los derechos de los obreros y trabajadores de esas empresas que no tienen la culpa del atraco bancario y a los cuales se toma imperioso proteger, y por otra, impedir que esa resolución pueda ser manipulada judicialmente por los oscuros intereses que ahora se ven afectados después de 10 años de total impunidad en el Ecuador.

Por lo mencionado y al amparo de lo dispuesto en el inciso segundo del Art. 25 del Reglamento de Funcionamiento de la Asamblea Constituyente, solicitamos se digne incluir en el orden del día el tratamiento del siguiente punto:

"Conocimiento y resolución del Mandato Constituyente sobre la resolución expedida por la Agencia de Garantía de Depósitos, Mandato AGD".

De la misma forma, agregamos a esta petición el proyecto de Mandato Constituyente motivo del cambio solicitado.

Con sentimientos de alta consideración y estima. .

Atentamente,

Marcos Martínez Flores R.

Ha. Alexandra Ocles.

182

ASAMBLEA CONSTITUYENTE

REPÚBLICA DEL ECUADOR

**EL PLENO DE LA
ASAMBLEA CONSTITUYENTE**

CONSIDERANDO:

Que, la Asamblea Constituyente en el artículo 1 del Mandato No. 1, aprobado en sesión del Pleno de 29 de noviembre de 2007 y publicado en el Suplemento del Registro Oficial No. 223 de viernes 30 de noviembre de 2007, asume y ejerce los PLENOS PODERES;

Que, el artículo 1 del Reglamento de Funcionamiento de la Asamblea Constituyente de 11 de diciembre de 2007, publicado en el Suplemento del Registro Oficial No. 236 de 20 de diciembre de 2007, dispone: *"La Asamblea Constituyente representa a la soberanía popular que radica en el pueblo ecuatoriano, y por su propia naturaleza está dotada de plenos poderes";*

Que, el artículo 2, numeral 2 del Reglamento de Funcionamiento de la Asamblea Constituyente, dispone: *"En el ejercicio de sus poderes, la Asamblea Constituyente aprobará...2. Mandatos Constituyentes: Decisiones y normas que expida la Asamblea Constituyente para el ejercicio de sus plenos poderes. Estos mandatos tendrán efecto inmediato, sin perjuicio de su publicación en el órgano respectivo",*

Que la quiebra del sistema financiero en los años 90 causó enormes pérdidas al Estado ecuatoriano, las mismas que fueron asumidas por todos los ecuatorianos, y que hasta la fecha no han logrado ser saldadas en su totalidad;

Que, la Agencia de Garantía de Depósitos, en su calidad de Juez de Coactiva, mediante Resolución AGD-UIO-GG-2008-12, del 8 de julio de 2008, con vista en las pérdidas estimadas de 661,5 millones de dólares, contra los ex-accionistas de Filanbanco S.A. ordenó la inmediata incautación de varios de sus bienes al tenor de lo dispuesto en el artículo 29 reformado de la Ley de Reordenamiento en Materia Económica en el área Tributario-Financiera;

Que, la Asamblea Constituyente, apoya las acciones que adoptan los poderes constituidos en la erradicación de toda forma de corrupción e impunidad así como la libertad de expresión en democracia, la cual no se verá afectada por esta medida que no tiene relación directa con la referida libertad;

Que, la Asamblea Constituyente, en ejercicio de sus Plenos Poderes y en aras de la paz social, está en la obligación de velar por la

183

estabilidad, derechos y garantías de los trabajadores y empleados de las empresas intervenidas por la Agencia de Garantía de Depósitos (AGD) mediante Resolución AGD-UIO-GG-2008-12, del 8 de julio de 2008; y,

En uso de sus atribuciones y facultades expide el siguiente:

MANDATO CONSTITUYENTE No. 13

Artículo 1.- Ratificar la plena validez legal de la Resolución AGD-UIO-GG-2008-12 del 8 de julio de 2008, en la que se ordena la incautación de los bienes de los ex accionistas y ex administradores de Filanbanco S.A., con la finalidad de devolver el dinero al Estado y a todos los ecuatorianos que aún permanecen perjudicados por la quiebra de dicho banco.

Artículo 2.- Declarar que la resolución AGD-UIO-GG-2008-12 de 8 de julio de 2008, expedida por el Gerente General de la Agencia de Garantía de Depósitos no es susceptible de acción de amparo constitucional u otra de carácter especial, y si de hecho se hubiere interpuesto, será inmediatamente archivada, sin que se pueda suspender o impedir el cumplimiento de la referida resolución. Los jueces o magistrados que avocaren conocimiento de cualquier clase de acción constitucional relativa a esta resolución y aquellas que se tomen para ejecutarla, implementarla o cumplirla a cabalidad, deberán inadmitirlas, bajo pena de destitución y sin perjuicio de la responsabilidad penal a la que hubiere lugar.

Artículo 3.- La AGD deberá aplicar el artículo 29 de la Ley de Reordenamiento en Materia Económica, sin excepción, a todos los administradores y accionistas de bancos que cerraron sus operaciones y pasaron a control de la AGD y que se encuentran incursos en la norma referida.

Artículo 4.- Precautelar la estabilidad de los trabajadores y empleados de las empresas intervenidas por la Agencia de Garantía de Depósitos (AGD) mediante Resolución AGD-UIO-GG-2008-12 de julio 8 de 2008.

DISPOSICIÓN FINAL

El presente Mandato es de obligatorio cumplimiento y en tal virtud, no será susceptible de queja, impugnación, acción de amparo, demanda, reclamo, criterio o pronunciamiento administrativo o judicial alguno y entrará en vigencia en forma inmediata, sin perjuicio de su publicación en la Gaceta Constitucional y/o en el Registro Oficial.

Notifíquese el contenido de este Mandato, al Presidente de la República,

ASAMBLEA CONSTITUYENTE

a los representantes de los poderes constituidos y al Gerente General de la Agencia de Garantía de Depósitos.

Dado y suscrito en el Centro Cívico *"Ciudad Alfaro"*, cantón Montecristi, provincia de Manabí de la República del Ecuador, a los nueve días del mes de julio de dos mil ocho.

FERNANDO CORDERO CUEVA
Presidente de la Asamblea Constituyente

DR. FRANCISCO VERGARA O.
Secretario

185

BANCO CENTRAL DEL ECUADOR

GERENCIA GENERAL

ARCHIVO

Quito, 12 de junio de 2000
SE-1462-2000   00 01867

Señora Doctora
Mariana Yépez de Velasco
Ministra Fiscal General del Estado
Ciudad

Firma:_____

Señora Ministra Fiscal General:

Ante el aparecimiento de un sinnúmero de noticias de prensa relativas a la utilización de los recursos otorgados por el Banco Central del Ecuador a Filanbanco a fines de 1998, es mi obligación poner en su conocimiento la información relacionada con dichas operaciones y el correspondiente análisis que en materia financiera el caso requiere, a fin confirmar la transparencia con la que siempre ha operado el Banco Central del Ecuador.

Antecedentes:

El panorama económico del país se caracterizó por un deterioro de la situación fiscal, agravada por la caída de los precios de exportación de petróleo, una reducción de flujos de financiamiento externo hacia el país, producto de la turbulencia financiera internacional creada por la crisis de los países asiáticos y del Brasil y una serie de desequilibrios internos ocasionados por los efectos de fenómenos naturales adversos.

Durante el año 1998 se registró una inflación anual de 43.4%, como resultado de la elevación del costo de transporte público, el encarecimiento de algunos bienes alimenticios, por el impacto del Fenómeno de El Niño y la eliminación de los subsidios a la energía eléctrica, al gas doméstico y la elevación del precio de los demás combustibles.

En cuanto al tipo de cambio, durante 1998 se efectuaron dos ajustes a la banda cambiaria, que permitieron reducir el comportamiento especulativo de los agentes económicos y mejorar la competitividad de los productos de exportación ecuatorianos en el contexto de una balanza comercial desfavorable.

186

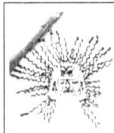

BANCO CENTRAL DEL ECUADOR

GERENCIA GENERAL

00 01867

FILANBANCO S.A. y FILANBANCO TRUST
SINTESIS CARTERA Y AVALES
MILES DE DOLARES

Variación de cartera on-shore	115,151
Venta de cartera	80,719
Avales activados	58,505
Total Operaciones Cartera	139,224
Recuperaciones	24,073

CONCLUSION

De la explicación detallada que queda consignada en el presente informe, señora Ministra Fiscal General, sobre los resultados del monitoreo realizado por el Banco Central a Filanbanco, durante el periodo indicado en que accedió a las líneas de liquidez del Banco Central, tanto mediante el seguimiento de tesorería cuanto el seguimiento de liquidez a nivel de balance, se puede inferir de la información proporcionada por Filanbanco que las necesidades de liquidez que tuvo dicha institución en ese periodo para honrar y pagar operaciones permitidas, fueron superiores al monto que efectivamente le concedió el Banco Central a dicha institución bancaria, por lo que ésta tuvo que utilizar necesariamente otras fuentes de recursos para cubrir esa diferencia en operaciones permitidas.

De hecho, del propio análisis se desprende que durante el mismo periodo, Filanbanco obtuvo recursos de otras fuentes distintas al Banco Central, todo lo cual ha llevado a que el Instituto Emisor actúe bajo la seguridad de que los recursos que estaba otorgando, y otorgó, fueron debidamente utilizados por la institución financiera prestataria para cubrir operaciones permitidas.

Aprovecho la oportunidad para reiterar a la señora Ministra Fiscal General mis sentimientos de alta estima y consideración.

Atentamente,
BANCO CENTRAL DEL ECUADOR

Miguel Dávila Castillo
GERENTE GENERAL

c.c. Dirección General Bancaria
      Asesoría Legal
      Secretaría General (2)

ENVIADO ANEXOS	☐
ENVIADO COPIAS	☑
SOBRE GENERAL	

BIBLIOGRAPHY

(Berchi A. et al. 2008, Crisis de Ecuador 2000: La dolarización y los indígenas [Ecuador's Crisis 2000: The dollarization of the indigenous] Available at www.caei.com.ar

Correa, Rafael 2004, "Ecuador: Dolarización y políticas alternativas. De absurdas dolarizaciones a uniones monetarias" [Ecuador: Dollarization and alternative policies. From absurd dollarization to monetary unions], Published by La Insignia. Ecuador, available at www.lainsignia.org

Guillen R, Arturo 2000, Efectos de la crisis asiática en América Latina. [Effects of the Asian crisis on Latin America] Comercio Exterior [Foreign Commerce], vol.50, No.7 Mexico.

Guerrero Vivanco, Walter 2003, Pedido de sobreseimiento a la Sala Penal de la Corte Suprema de Justicia [Petition for dismissal to the Penal Chambers of the Supreme Court of Justice]. Mimeographed document.

Jimeno, Ramon 2006, La culpa del Inocente: el caso de Roberto Isaías D. [The guilt of the Innocent: the case of Roberto Isaias D.] Miami: Jack Sasoon

Larrea Holguin, Juan 2003, Un análisis jurídico sobre el caso Filanbanco [A legal analysis of the Filanbanco Case]. Mimeographed document;

Zuniga, Nieves 2000, Ecuador en Crisis [Ecuador in Crisis]. Available at www.fuhem.es

http://filanbancocase.com

www.caei.ar

www.cidob.org/es

www.comisionanticorrupcion.gov.ec

www.derechoecuador.com

www.diccionariobiograficoecuador.com

www.diario-expreso.com

www.ecuadorinmediato.com

www.elecuatoriano.com

www.eluniverso.com

www.explored.com.ec

www.hoy.com.ec

http://report.globalintegrity.org/Ecuador